NICHE

A Book to Reshape Your Career

Poonam Singh

IP Singh

Printed in India

IndiePress

ISBN: 978-93-6045-690-0

First Printing, 2025

IndiePress

A division of Nasadiya Technologies Private Ltd.

Koramangala, Bangalore

Karnataka-560029

http://indiepress.in/

Edited By: Ridham Bassi

Typesetting By: MAPS systems

Publishing Consultant: Rechal Fernandes

Book Cover Design by Sankhashubro Nath

Also by the same author

-poonampowerquotes

Transforming Life's Blues Into Bliss

To my beloved father, Late Shri Yogendra Pal Singh ji, whose work ethics and passion for his craft have been the driving force and inspiration behind writing this book.

To all the young job aspirants and professionals who are striving to shine brightly in their careers, despite the challenges they face.

Disclaimer

The information presented in this book is for educational and general guidance purpose, and hope will inspire you. Remember that individual results may vary and no guarantees are made for a specific outcome.

Contents

Disclaimer ix
Introduction xiii
Preface xv
Acknowledgements xvii
A Letter To Readers xix

Chapter One: Job 1

Chapter Two: Talent 15

Chapter Three: First Impression And Personality 29

Chapter Four: Manners And Etiquette 41

Chapter Five: Hard Work 51

Chapter Six: Professional Attitude 63

Chapter Seven: Imbibing Qualities 81

Chapter Eight: Yes Man 101

Chapter Nine: Self Appraisal 117

Chapter Ten: How To Get A Job?

(Part 1) 133

How To Get A Job?

(Part 2) 151

Chapter Eleven: Modern Work Culture 163

About Authors 181

Connect with me 183

Introduction to "Niche: A Book to Reshape Your Career"

As seasoned professionals with distinguished careers, we've experienced the thrill of achievement and the value of strategic decision-making. Poonam, a celebrated educationist and accomplished author, has left an indelible mark on the world of science and English education. IP Singh, a civil engineer and gold medallist, has scaled the heights of corporate success as COO of a prominent infrastructure company in India.

United by our passion for learning and personal growth, we frequently engage in thought-provoking discussions on education, science, and societal impact. Our conversations often circle back to the challenges faced by young individuals in today's fast-paced world.

Moved by a shared desire to empower the next generation, we've collaborated on this book to provide valuable insights and guidance. "Niche" is designed to help young adults navigate the complexities of career choices, cultivate essential skills, and unlock their full potential.

Within these pages, we share our expertise, experiences, and perspectives to inspire and equip you to:

Rethink your study goals and career aspirations

Develop strategic skills for personal and professional success

Make informed decisions about your educational path

Build a fulfilling and impactful career

Join us on this transformative journey as we explore the intersection of passion, purpose, and profession.

Best regards,
Poonam and IP Singh

PREFACE

When we turn the leaves of our life's book, we find that our journey throughout has been that of a 'learner' who never held back from focusing on education. Education has played a pivotal role in shaping our lives.

When you have made your presence felt in the world, it's when you have achieved something good or great in your life. That thing could be big, or it could be small, and that hardly makes a difference to the world, but what makes a difference to you is of the utmost concern. This is because whatever you achieved in your life should have given a sense of fulfillment to you somewhere down the line.

So, broadly speaking, the thing which gives you the most satisfaction is what makes you happy.

Supporting our statement, we confess that our achievements in our jobs were the elixir of our lives. We call it the most satisfying thing because it was giving us food for thought and real-life experiences that helped us shape our lives. We always dreamt of a perfect life, a perfect family, and in the zest of having a perfect family life, we were blessed with two sons. But the studies never ended for us. We gave leeway to our creative and appropriately educated minds and became a teacher (eventually the school coordinator at an early stage of the job) and COO of an acclaimed company in the private sector, respectively.

We got ample opportunities to flutter our wings of knowledge to the fullest in our work spheres.

With the profundity of knowledge and dedication to our work, we very soon were able to 'carve our niche' in our workplaces. We upheld the most challenging tasks assigned to us with the greatest precision and responsibility. All these attributes became our stepping stones in the writing of this book. With our backgrounds as professionals, we were filled with experiences of what challenges and hurdles one faces when going to work, whether in an institute or an office. We had a bird's eye view over the nuances of the job sphere. By way of this book, we wish to share our job experiences with the readers, especially young adults, who are in the process of finding a job or looking for some guidance or an expert's advice on how to navigate, grow, and excel in their job. This book will serve as a ready toolkit for carving a niche in one's workplace.

Penning down this book was a total recapture of our lives as working professionals. We relived our journey as working professionals as we jotted down topic after topic and chapter after chapter of this book.

There were challenges while penning down this book, such as going down memory lane to put forth some true incidents. We had to review our old papers related to our jobs and analyze data contained in them so that we could figure out a sequential flow of chapters and incorporate actual data picked up from our job expertise.

As we started penning down incidents, data, and little tasks, which we beautifully transformed into big achievements, we almost caught the chords of how a job should be done and how working professionals should conduct themselves in order to bring out the best in them.

Today, Poonam has retired from the job but not from work, while I.P. Singh stands tall and strides ahead in his active professional role.

Acknowledgements

Writing the acknowledgments for a book is both an exciting and challenging task. The journey of bringing a book to life—from its inception to completion—is shaped by the involvement and support of so many people. There is always a risk of missing someone whose contribution, though behind the scenes, has been crucial in the process.

This book would not have been possible without my time spent working at the school, and the invaluable support I received from I.P. Singh, who was instrumental in the administrative aspects. Both of us are deeply indebted to our colleagues and mentors for their continuous encouragement and guidance, which has shaped our careers and ultimately brought this book to life.

Throughout this journey, we have been each other's unwavering support, especially when we faced moments of writer's block, struggling with words, ideas, or experiences to include in the book.

A special thanks to our sons, Sahil and Pravar, who, despite being in New York, have been our trailblazers, guides, and constant sources of inspiration.

Our heartfelt gratitude goes to our daughters-in-law, Ruth and Aishwarya, for their technical support, especially in navigating apps like Canva and handling contemporary social media challenges.

We are immensely grateful to the editor of this book, Ms. Ridham Bassi, whose careful scrutiny and valuable feedback helped the book capture its essence.

Our sincere thanks go to Mr. Sankhashubro Nath, our senior designer, for creating the stunning book cover. It's worth noting that Mr. Nath's two other book covers were recently selected for the "Longlist of the 10th edition of Oxford Bookstore Book Cover Awards."

We would also like to thank Ms. Rechal Fernandes, our publishing consultant, for coordinating the entire publishing process and ensuring the timely release of the book.

Our deepest appreciation extends to the entire Indie Press team for their steadfast support throughout the publication process.

Lastly, but most importantly, we are forever indebted to our readers. Your genuine feedback and honest reviews make our book what it is, turning it into an unforgettable read. You are the reason our writing has meaning, and we are truly grateful.

A Letter to Readers

Dear Readers,

Books have always been the best way to speak from the heart, and today, that's exactly what I'm doing.

After the publication of my first book in 2023, I was ecstatic. The feeling of holding your own work, your own creation, in your hands is beyond words. It's like embracing your thoughts, your story, and your experiences in a tangible form. When I first read my own script in the book—from page to page—it sent a shiver down my spine. It was as if I were reading the very authentic thoughts of someone truly acclaimed. Even though I knew I had written them, I was still captivated by the magic of seeing those words printed in a book.

I mention this to you because I want to share the journey I've been on. I began as an intuitive writer, but along the way, the process has been filled with invaluable learnings and accomplishments. My first book was recognized as an Amazon Bestseller. This achievement inspired me to write again, and this time, I wanted to reflect on my experiences as a teacher and school coordinator—my first love and passion. For me, writing has been a way of sharing my thoughts and experiences—some of which are very real.

In this book, "NICHE," I am joined by my husband, I.P. Singh, who is a celebrated scholar in his own right. As a co-author, he brings his immense knowledge and valuable experiences to the book. A renowned civil engineer, he is also the iconic COO of a reputed infrastructure company in India. This book marks his debut as a co-author, and his contributions have provided a strong foundation for the chapters, especially Chapter 11, which is entirely his. This chapter is a must-read for young job entrants and job seekers.

Our advice to you, the readers, is to approach this book with the intention of achieving something meaningful. May it serve as a cornerstone for your career and personal growth.

Best wishes,

Poonam Singh and I.P. Singh

Chapter One
Job

PURPOSE OF JOB

"What is the purpose of doing a job?" This question might sound funny to anyone. Most of us will laugh it off and say, obviously, we work to earn some bucks, to earn a livelihood. We work to fulfil our basic needs and to endure the stresses of life. Having food on our plate every day is our first basic need. Secondly, we need clothes to cover our bodies, and thirdly, we need shelter—a home where we can live safely and securely. Who can deny the importance of these rudimentary requirements to lead a normal life? On the other hand, there is another side to this story where you'll find that people may still work even when their basic needs are fulfilled already.

So, if you research a little on the 'Big Question'—i.e., what the purpose of doing a job is—you will find that-

> "There is a great chunk of people who are working for not just earning a livelihood."

Doesn't it sound curious and a little off-track? Then, what could be the other possible reasons they are working for? Before we reflect on this 'Big Question.' we need to look left, right, and centre, i.e., at the social setup in which we live. We'll have to turn to our past values, our gender, the region where we are born, our exposure to the world, family ethics, the form of education, and so on. We'll have to look back on these aspects of society because they impact how or what profession we'll finally indulge in the future.

But here, I must mention one very critical point, which is about your INNER SELF: whether you OPEN up to anyone with the greatest ease, whether you are CURIOUS to know the universe from your heart, and whether you WANT to make a difference in this universe. These points about the

'Inner Self' have the power to transform a person's life from scratch to affluence. They act as 'Natural Motivators' to one's inner being, playing a major role in deciding one's job or profession. We'll discuss this in later chapters, including how these personal attributes are also crucial to 'CARVING YOUR NICHE' in your profession.

THE BIG QUESTION

Now, we are in a better position to ask ourselves some questions to somehow relate to this BIG QUESTION—i.e., what is our purpose in doing a job? When I researched this big question, I was aimed at by a volley of questions, which I have put in the form of statements as follows (I hope you would also agree with at least 70% of them):

- I need to find a job to support my family. (financial need)
- I am looking for a pastime. (casual, pastime need)
- I must get a job because I studied so much. (educational need)
- I am competent and highly qualified, so I must get a deserving job. (competitive need)
- I am so creative and talented; I must work. (creative need)
- I am ambitious and have a lot of expectations from myself; I find satisfaction in work only. (ambitious need)
- I am talented and capable of setting examples; I must work. (expression need)
- Everyone works, so I must also work. (social recognition need)
- Everyone in my family works, so I must work as well. (family recognition need)

- I should be highly placed so that I am respected in society. (social need)
- If I don't work, I won't be able to find my soulmate or get married. (marital need)
- I want to live a life that goes beyond fulfilling basic needs, so I must work. (rich life need)
- We'll be role models for our children, so we must work. (setting standards for children's needs)
- I need 'food for the brain.' so I must work. (cognitive need)

There can be innumerable reasons to answer this 'Big Question.' Life is so complex, with manifold needs and circumstances that unfold with every passing human. Therefore, the purpose of doing a job is multiple; it's not only for financial reasons but for many other reasons in modern society.

> In any case, whatever the nature of the need, every need is basic and topmost for the concerned individual.

So, if a person wants to work for whatever reason, he or she must get a job to keep themselves engaged in the way they want.

KIND OF JOB

"If one has to work, what kind of job should one get to be fairly satisfied and successful?" Before answering this next 'Tickling Question.' I will take you on a random journey into my life. Born to an eminent electrical engineer father, I was fortunate enough to have been born with a certain appreciable degree of scientific aptitude. Following my father's footsteps, my inclination toward science was evident from the early years of my student life. I grew up as a proficient biology student, and my path was clear: if I ever took up a job in my future life, it was going to be related to science. This was so well-infused into my destiny that, as a result, I became a science teacher.

So, this was the job I took upon my 'Education Need.' and it was totally in sync with the subjects I pursued as a student.

> This was the traditional outcome of my studies, which shaped my destiny to become a science teacher. Here, it may be noted that I adhered to the core subject of my father, i.e., science (though the branch of science that I pursued was biology). So, this story relates to numerous individuals who opt for the jobs of their parents or forefathers. In a way, this is a very natural routine outcome when we try to find an answer to the 'Tickling Question' we talked about in the beginning.

Apart from opting for parents' professions or businesses, one can explore numerous diverse fields of work these days. There is an infinite avenue of open studies and, subsequently, of work that caters to the interests, aspirations, and skills of individuals. These days, studies are interest-oriented, and so people find it easy to get a 'job of their choice' in their subsequent life.

In the past, there were three basic streams of study: Science, Commerce, and Humanities, with an emphasis on related regular core subjects. Now, the courses of study offered in the above three streams are multiple, with abundant scope in each of these fields.

For example, there are separate sets of courses for fashion design, management jobs, data science jobs, 'analyst jobs, mass communication jobs, and so on—the list is unending. There are even 'career counsellors' these days who help us decipher our choice of career. It's a great privilege that our society, our parents, and our teachers show flexibility of mind and promote us in every way to make the right choice for our career.

It's hard to believe, but it's a fact today that girls are no longer the unprivileged gender; rather, girls are showing equal interest in opting for a career. They have extended their arms to those jobs and embraced them with full vigour and vitality, which were once considered the territory of boys. And our society is supportive of this change.

SWITCHING JOB CATEGORIES

"Do we have a future in other categories of jobs, or in other words, can we go for diversified jobs or switch jobs at any stage of life?" Clearly, the answer is YES. I can say this with so much conviction because my life story gives you the firsthand answer. From a science teacher to becoming an author, the journey was filled with anxiety, determination, and a rush of emotions, coupled with performing different roles in life with equal aplomb.

I became a published author in the self-help genre, a field quite distant from the scientific temperament that I possessed. And now, I'm equally excited about authoring this second script of mine. So, another thing becomes clear from this example: whatever course of study we might have pursued in our early years of life, there is always a door open for a totally different field of study, even in the later stage of our life.

There are many reasons why you may succeed in diverse fields. To count a few, I enumerate here some for the record:

- You may have a 'passion' that is different from the one you are pursuing currently.
- You might have followed traditional courses during your student life while your 'interests' were different.
- You might have had 'pressures' from family and society to choose the so-called 'elite' subjects to be securely placed in a job.
- You might be 'afraid' of not doing so well if you change your job field at a later stage of life.

> So, whatever the reason for changing the category of your job, you can go for it, but this time it should be the JOB OF YOUR INTEREST.

You can go for diverse fields; the only condition is that it should interest you, and when you give your heart and soul to it, it should support you in eclectic ways. Age should never be a barrier to switching job categories. If you feel there isn't much financial risk or otherwise in switching, you must go ahead with it. Most of the time, we stick to the same job category because we can't afford a 'switch' (perhaps because we aren't financially sound enough). In that case, you can follow your light-hearted, passionate job along with your main job (please ensure that your company allows you to take up a side job).

Here, I would like to mention that this is a tech era, and children are awakened and passionate about pursuing their talent in computers. They are showcasing their skills and profound knowledge in these areas. The children want lateral outlets for their vast knowledge, acumen, and interest. These days, we have seen young children making beautiful, convenient, and user-friendly apps that cater to a variety of our needs and ease our lives. So, if a child has such pursuits, I think he or she should go for it along with his or her current job if possible or needed.

To support my point that you can switch job categories at any stage of life and still be established and successful, I quote the names of Indian authors like Chetan Bhagat and Ashneer Grover. They switched from engineering to becoming authors. Foreign authors like J.K. Rowling, James Clear, and Yuval Noah Harari all switched from different fields of study to becoming authors. They are all celebrated authors of great acclaim.

A JOB HALF DONE IS AS GOOD AS NONE

The above is a famous quote by Luke Granger, and how aptly it has been said.

Once you're in a profession or a job, you can't do it half-heartedly. A job done with little to no interest or enthusiasm will lead to a 'bad job done.' What could be the repercussions of doing a job without fully committing to it? This question needs to be answered in one's mind before he or she starts expecting results. Here, I have derived a few ill effects of doing a job without fuelling the mind to the extent it should have been:

- No applause for your work.
- Losing perks and promotions.
- No dependency on your work or yourself.
- Your work is not given due regard.
- You feel dissatisfied.
- You feel low and unenergetic.
- You're unable to 'Carve a Niche' in your workplace.

I'll explain this to you with an example from my life. I started my YouTube channel, SCIENCE BUG, by Poonam Singh, without much clarity in my mind about how to proceed, what kind of videos to prepare, or which topics from the vast and diverse spheres of the subject—science—to take. In a way, I started off without giving much thought to such issues, which appeared trivial to me. Sometimes, I posted videos on teaching-learning techniques; other times, I chose a random topic for a random grade, and so on. I was not channelled, guided and sincere in my approach. As a result, I had very few subscribers and very few views, mostly from my close-knit circle.

Then, I decided to publish videos on biology topics from the Grade 10 course book and follow a structured course of study with a targeted approach toward teaching biology. I started amassing good responses over time. Although the struggle continued, I now have a mindset where success appears inevitable to me.

> So, it's clear that to achieve success or to 'leave a mark in your work sphere.' you need to be optimally keen and enthusiastic, decisive with a roadmap, begin work with a focused mindset, and be ***fuelled*** enough to hit the nail on the head.

Once you're geared up with a mindset where your 'goals and roadmap' to achieve them are crystal clear, success will not be another story. You'll be a confident person who will come out with flying colours every time. You'll be noticed and valued in the eyes of your supervisors. You'll surely become one of the most dependable persons in your workplace. With your proactive and concerted decisions, you're bound to achieve a key position in your workplace.

Thus, we see that when the job is done with precision and prudence, the results are overwhelming and far-reaching. This is one of the greatest ways to 'carve a niche' for yourself in your work sphere. This method requires dedication, and you may even have to sweat blood to achieve great results; it could be time-consuming, varying from individual to individual, but this method has no substitute for it; IT HAS NO SHORTCUT. By sweating blood, I don't mean to say that you have to compromise your physical and mental health, but rather, YOU NEED TO WORK SMARTLY, MAKING THE BEST POSSIBLE USE OF YOUR SKILLS.

MAKING A DIFFERENCE IS IMPORTANT

When the job is done wholeheartedly, you are bound to make a difference. THIS IS DESTINED! How should I proceed, or how much should I indulge myself in my job to be productive? This is the only question that should keep nagging you and thus keep you going on your way to 'carve a niche.' The very basic factor that gives a prime answer to the above question depends on "HOW YOU VISUALISE YOUR INNER SELF" (We talked about the 'inner self' at the beginning of this chapter). For this, you can ask the following questions to yourself:

- Am I positive, prudent, purposeful, and practical?
- Am I strong enough to face challenges?
- Am I hard-working and above average in my chosen field?
- Am I honest and dedicated?
- Am I amiable and good at PR?
- Do I enjoy my work?

Asking these questions will prepare you to undertake a job where you also desire to 'carve a niche' for yourself.

> By making you ask these questions, I never mean that only when you score 100% in answering them that you can pick up a job. Asking these questions encourages you to "GIVE YOUR BEST FOR ACHIEVING THE BEST."

Even if you don't score 100% at the early stage of your job, you don't have to RECLINE IN REST, thinking that this job is not your cup of tea. Only a handful of people are born with all the above qualities. Most people acquire many of these attributes as they mature and when they work constantly toward them.

These are some key questions that, if you ask yourself, will help you evaluate, i.e., they will help you to ANALYSE/ VISUALISE YOUR INNER SELF. Now, what is this 'Inner Self' that we're talking about constantly? The inner self is your inherent mind, body, and soul makeup, which makes you the person that you are. Your 'Inner Self' will drive you through your day-to-day challenges and obstacles. Your 'Inner Self' will lead you on your path of life with ease or difficulty, happily or annoyingly, joyfully or hastily, lethargically or eagerly, with fret or with grit. Your 'Inner Self' will guide you in all your decision-making and interactions with peers/ colleagues. So, knowing your Inner Self is crucial. In short, YOUR INNER SELF IS THE HARBINGER OF YOUR ACTIONS.

Your Inner Self can be modified

Yes, it's true! By practising self-realisation and self-control and rising above the existing 'Inner Self,' the 'Inner Self' can be changed to suit critical life circumstances. It's not that you can change your 'Inner Self,' at the tick of a clock, but with rigorous practice, it can be modified to a great extent until it becomes a habit. Once you're the beholder of a great 'Inner Self.' you can achieve the desired success in your job and other aspects of your life.

ACTIVITY 1

My Roadmap to 'Carve a Niche'

1. I do my job to..
   ....
   ....
   ....
2. I took a traditional job (Please tick). Yes/No............
   ....
   ....
   ....
3. I switched jobs because...
   ....
   ....
   ....
4. My expectations from the job are................................
   ....
   ....
5. I delved deep into my job by...................................
   ....
   ....
   ....
6. My 'Inner Self' supports me as I'm.........................
   ....
   ....
   ....

Chapter Two
Talent

TALENT IS NOT TAUGHT

It has been very well explained in the previous chapters that one must do the job wholeheartedly; one must make a difference in the workplace by standing out. Our 'Inner Self' is very much responsible for achieving all this success. Apart from the 'Inner Self.' there is another feature that overshadows all the others, and THAT IS YOUR TALENT.

Talent is an innate quality or ability that one possesses from birth. Every individual is born unique in their ways and mannerisms, abilities and capabilities, conceptions and perceptions, detailing and analysing their weaknesses or inhibitions, and strengths. So, if one is born with a fixed set of talents and abilities, then one's career or preferences shouldn't have been fixed right at the time of birth! But then why is a child made to study all subjects right from elementary school? This is because we can never predict what profession a child will choose when they grow up, even though their choices and preferences start becoming evident at an early age.

So, we can conclude that:

Although we are indeed driven by our instincts (which are innate) to a great extent, external factors like family profession, school education, peer influence, teacher influence on contemporary subjects, and many other external influences also play a major role in shaping one's talents, attitudes, and skills.

So, "What exactly do we mean by saying that a person is very talented?"
A Talented person has some intense inherent qualities and some intense external qualities that have influenced them throughout their nurturing. This is the most probable answer that one can derive from reading so far. Let's gain insight into the real meaning of talent by reading this incident:

The daughter of a friend of mine was an excellent artist as a child and was awarded many times for her talent in 'art.' Besides, she was interested in other subjects like math and English. Her talent for 'art' was evident even when she graduated from college, but the subject she pursued in her later life was math, and she became an accomplished CA. She pursued her other talent, i.e., 'art.' as a passion, a hobby, and a favourite pastime.

So, it's quite evident from this INSTANCE that the girl had a talent for 'art.' and she also had either an inherent or an acquired talent for math. Whatever the reason, we can guess the following things about a person's talent:

- A person may possess talents in more than one field of mental expression.
- A person may bear many cognitive, artistic, or behavioral talents at the same time.
- A person talented in one field may not take it up as their profession.
- A person may choose the talent in life that is more productive.
- Our talents also help us earn a living.
- One talent might be career-oriented, and another might be passion-oriented.

TALENTS CAN BE MODIFIED

Now, the next question that comes to our mind is: "Can talents that one has naturally—whether career-oriented or passion-oriented—be modified to some extent at least?" Certainly, talents can be modified to a great extent to fulfil the demands of a job in order to 'carve a niche for yourself.'

Let's understand 'how.' and for this, we'll take an example. When I was working in a school as a science teacher, teaching science was not my only purview, but with the world moving towards technology, I had to adapt technology in my teaching. Technology has become an inseparable part of my job. You must be wondering what a science teacher or any other subject teacher has to do with technology. Most of us think that science or any subject other than 'computers' at the school level can be taught with a whiteboard and a marker and, at most, by performing certain practicals. So, "Where does technology come into play?"

> Recalling that teaching and technology can't be separated, for that matter, any field of work—be it banking, grocery shops, cinema ticketing, air ticketing, police stations, or any office work—none is possible without technology in the modern world.

So, by hook or crook, to remain in sync with the modern world, you need to modify your talents and acquire new ones. Teaching leads the way in adapting technology with the advent of smart boards, e-books, use of PowerPoint presentations, etc. Not only that, but technology also took over the making and designing of worksheets, uploading marks, online results, students' data record-keeping, school purchase inventory, the record of books in the library, and so on—the manifestations are innumerable.

So, I hope that after reading this example, you'll agree that talents can be modified to different degrees based on professional requirements and one's adaptability to the changing world. This kind of adaptability may not be a cakewalk for many, but with a flexible attitude and mental receptiveness, such modifications in one's talents are possible. Such a modification calls for a lot of diligence and hard work. Only then can one get the desired results, which will directly impact one's ability to 'carve one's niche.' I hope you agree with me that it's important to carve your niche in your workplace because that is the direct route to your progress and, eventually, your success.

STRATEGIES TO MODIFY YOUR TALENTS

Every field of study is a stepwise, well-curated process. Every field of study has its own scientific ways to proceed through its well-defined course of action. In other words, every field of study is systematic, with well-defined methods to learn or grasp it and come out with feasible solutions. So, since we are talking about MODIFYING TALENTS here, I should be able to define it tangibly.

Here are some well-thought-out strategies to modify one's talents:

- Put in a lot of effort to learn a new skill, which is a form of talent. This makes me recall a quote by Tim Notke, a basketball coach, which stands so apt here:
- "Hard work beats talent when talent doesn't work hard."
- Enhancing the skill or talent first is the need of the hour.
- Opt for a short-term or part-time, online or offline course/coaching to develop the talent or skill.
- There is no age for learning. So, don't be disheartened to learn a new skill/talent at a later stage.

> - If something still deters you from learning a new skill or talent, then make up your mind to switch your job to the JOB OF YOUR INTEREST.

I have derived these strategies from my own personal experiences. Nonetheless, YOUR EXPERIENCES ARE YOUR BEST GUIDEBOOKS. I started to incorporate technology into my teaching at the age of 45. The beginning wasn't easy; nevertheless, there was no way to abstain from it. We felt a lacuna in our teaching whenever we prepared worksheets or question papers. The worksheets didn't look appealing until they were typed and enhanced with images taken from free online image sites like Shutterstock, etc. The pages of report cards for students never looked presentable until they had typed text about students' performance. When the prints came out in colour, the headings and images lit up in an attractive manner. The effect of technology was beautifully etched on paper and in every nook and corner of the study. Not only did the papers look pleasing, but the work also became easier with computers. Any information or record became available at the 'click of the keys.' My experience with technology was like that of a child becoming amused, enthusiastic, and thrilled when he first started to walk.

After spending many years with technology, we became almost fully dependent on the thing we were so scared of in the beginning. So, I'm of the firm opinion that one must be adaptive to any kind of change because NEW IS NOVICE AND FOR ONE's EASE.

Nonetheless, this explains my point very well: we should make constant efforts to modify our talents so that we're able to 'carve a niche' in our work sphere.

UNFOLD YOUR STRENGTHS OVER YOUR WEAKNESSES

"I have no special talent. I am only passionately curious."

— Albert Einstein

Every person has one talent or another. They may be good at one or many things at the same time (this has been discussed at length in the previous chapter). On the other hand, there can be a few areas where they may lack completely. No person is born PERFECT. The strong and weak qualities of a person go hand-in-hand. One mustn't cry or complain about one's weaknesses but rather accept the way one is. Realise your qualities and act accordingly. Your strong areas will guide you in choosing your path or career, while the weak areas need to be strengthened or can be sidelined. If you make a 'mountain out of a molehill' of your weaknesses, you'll end up confused, lost, reticent, dejected, and unhappy. So, forget or put aside your weaknesses and focus on enhancing your strengths. You can use your strong talents to empower yourself and win over your weaknesses.

Ponder over the following statements by different people:

- I'm inquisitive.
- I'm very loquacious.
- I'm an extrovert.
- I'm good at debating.
- I'm a good listener.
- I'm quite confident.
- I'm very creative.
- I'm a passionate learner.

- I'm a good speaker.
- I can interact very well with people.
- I'm studious.
- I'm well-behaved and disciplined.
- I'm very positive.
- I'm trustworthy and dependable.
- I'm honest and a person of principles.
- I'm shy and introverted.
- I'm wise and decisive.
- I have a pleasing personality.
- I'm hard-working.
- I'm fond of music.
- I'm good at sports.
- I'm good at art.
- I can impress people.
- I talk sense.
- It takes me time to gel with people.
- I can make my point effectively.
- I'm very helpful and enjoy doing it.
- I have good moral conduct and value ethical working.
- I love gardening, reading the newspaper, cooking, anchoring, writing poems and short stories, and reading comics and magazines.
- I'm a good storyteller.
- I'm good at dramatics.

- I'm competitive and ambitious.
- I get upset easily.
- I'm authoritative and didactic.

This list of such human manifestations will be unending because human behaviour is unbounded. The list shows that a person may be good at one or many things at a time while also having weaknesses. The list shows more positive qualities and only a few negative ones, which suggests that we should focus more on our strengths rather than our weaknesses.

My objective in preparing this list was just to show that humans have varied physical, mental, and behavioural traits. From this list, you might relate to a few, even though there are many qualities not mentioned here. This list highlights some of the very basic attributes or talents of a person rather than delving deep into the 'skills.'

Talents and skills are attributes that are achieved through different means. Talent is largely an inherent gift, while skill can be acquired externally by consistently working on it. We will discuss 'skills' more later in the book.talented

Now, let us try to explain whatever we learned so far with the help of the following example:

In a previous example, a girl who was good at art and math took up math to satisfy her career-oriented talent and pursued art to satisfy her passion-oriented talent. In this case, both her talents became her strengths in life.

I didn't tell you about her weaknesses at that time. The same girl was not equally comfortable with science subjects. As a result, she chose the 'commerce stream.' gave up on the 'science stream.' and chose to become a CA later in her life.

She was also good at English, which enhanced her career with amazing PR skills.

This girl didn't worry about her weakness in science subjects; instead, she honed the other skills and talents (math and related subjects like accountancy, business studies, etc.) that she was good at.

This is a clear example of how focusing on strengths over weaknesses is purely based on the 'choice of academic subjects' opted commonly by students.

You may witness several similar examples around you or read about them in newspapers. There are many interesting examples from the entertainment world, like in Bollywood, where you see that some very talented actors initially pursued different fields of study before becoming popular actors.

There are a few examples in recent times where some beauty pageant winners were pursuing medicine.

These examples are enough to prove my point that a person may be good in more than one field and may also have some weaknesses in other areas. The best approach is to identify and hone one's strengths while carrying them when choosing a career. At the same time, it is best to overlook or ignore the weaknesses rather than carry them as a burden.

> If people are born with certain weaknesses, they also carry a number of strengths that allow them to thrive. So, the key takeaway is: STRENGTHEN YOUR STRENGTHS AND BEAR WITH YOUR WEAKNESSES.

ACTIVITY 2

My Roadmap to 'Carve a Niche'

1. I show talent in fields like..
....
....
....

2. My career-oriented talent is..
....
....
....

3. My passion-oriented talent is..
....
....
....

4. I have modified/honed this talent to do better in my job..
....
....
....
....

5. I have worked on these strengths to choose my job
....
....
....

6. I have ignored these weaknesses to carry on confidently with my job..
....
....
....
....
....

Chapter Three

First Impression And Personality

FIRST IMPRESSION IS THE LAST IMPRESSION

"You never get a second chance to make
a good first impression."

- Will Rogers

Well! Talent is one significant portal to one's career or job, as we have all understood so far.

"What is a first impression?" The immediate conclusion we draw or the instant perception we form about a person when meeting them for the first time is the FIRST IMPRESSION. Have you ever experienced this? You all must have at some point in your life.

First impressions are a very important factor that builds your charisma for the other person. A first impression lasts almost forever.

Don't you think it is very crucial to talk about first impressions when we are discussing 'carving a niche?' If you succeed in creating a good first impression, half the job in procuring a position or getting into a business deal is done.

I worked as a coordinator in my school and had opportunities to interview or take demos from some teachers. I was indeed influenced and won over by some candidates/ teachers so much by their first impression that I hardly gave heed to other aspects. Here, I would like to share those things that made me a fan of some of those teachers:

- **Appearance**: This included the way the teacher dressed, how they carried themselves, overall hygiene, and their aura.

- **Personality**: This included not only their overall appearance but also the way they communicated, whether they looked confident, whether they could make eye contact, and whether they stood with an upright posture.
- **Body Language**: Body language says a lot about a person's manners and mannerisms. It was very important for me to judge teachers because this one thing resonates with others.
- **Communication Skills**: This includes not only the command over the language but also the effectiveness of the speech—i.e., whether it was spoken in a pleasant tone, with clarity, and with proper stresses and pauses. As an observer during the demos of the teachers, whenever I was enticed by their speech, I completely overlooked their looks.

Their first impression lasts forever; this is my personal experience. However, a bad first impression certainly leaves a negative impact, and it might take quite a long time for that person to get over that impression. That person would have to work hard on all the above-mentioned parameters to clear out that negative image and be in the good books of their boss.

> The first impression is created within the first few seconds of meeting a person, so you can fully imagine its worth.

TIPS TO MAKE A GOOD FIRST IMPRESSION

Till now, we have learned that it is crucial to make a good first impression on the concerned person because this tells about 80% of your story and is etched in the mind of the observer, forming a critical image of you which lasts for a long time. Of course, to maintain this image, you need to work hard consistently and prove your mettle.

Here are some strong tips that will help you create a positive first impression:

- As soon as you meet your boss, 'shake hands' firmly and look 'directly in the eye' (eye contact is very important and shows that you are confident).
- Introduce yourself with the greatest regard for your boss, and at the same time, remain polite in speech.
- Your 'posture' and 'gestures' make a big difference. Keep your posture tall and engage in friendly talk while keeping yourself cool and composed. At the same time, maintain the necessary professional distance between the boss (your senior) and you.
- Throughout your interaction, show your interest in the conversation by nodding your head in confirmation.
- Refrain from non-contextual talks and be precise (you may elaborate on the topic if required) during the conversation.
- Dress smartly in formal attire with proper grooming, including good personal hygiene and polished shoes. Refrain from yawning at any time.

- Speak confidently, maintaining high standards of speech. At the same time, avoid boasting. Your communication skills play a significant role in making a good first impression, so make good use of that.
- Refrain from overshadowing, demeaning, or belittling your boss's stature.
- Refrain from cracking irrelevant or obscene jokes. Instead, foster a good, healthy, congenial, and stress-free environment using subtle gestures or mild humour.
- Keep your mobile on silent and refrain from picking up calls.

A 'good first impression' can never be created artificially; it's either something you carry intrinsically at your behest or something you have worked hard enough to develop your personality over time.

GREAT PERSONALITY—A PRECURSOR TO CARVING A NICHE

"If life is a race, looks will help you win only sprints, while your good personality helps you win long marathons."

- Good Vitae

As laymen, we all think that personality is all about looks; the fact is that it is an attribute much beyond that. Looks can engage you for a few seconds and may also succeed in creating some amount of impression. However, personality is something people carry far and beyond wherever they go and whoever they meet. So, personality is that engaging quality that keeps you glued to and mesmerised by that person until you part ways. It's a magnetic phenomenon, and the charm it carries overrules even the brightest answers given by a passerby. Such is the impact of a great personality.

Can we define personality by one or two factors about it? The answer is 'No.' Personality is an amalgamation of a whole lot of human attributes. Apart from behavioural, intellectual, wit, and communicational skills, some attributes are so subtle that they will take you by surprise, and you will need to tickle your brain. Here are a few I would love to quote:

- To possess an impressive personality, learn to express yourself.
- Always be genuine and be yourself.
- You need not submit to others so easily until you get a satisfactory response.
- Be different, be unique, be yourself.
- You can be the change the society or the world looks for.
- You need to stand tall and make a place for yourself in society.

HOW TO BE ON THE OTHER SIDE OF THE TABLE WHERE YOUR PERSONALITY REBOUNDS?

"Personality begins where comparison leaves off."

- Anonymous

To be on the other side of the table is a 'Herculean task.' which is achievable by raising your personality to that level. Now, I will give you a few tips to mould/enhance/improve your personality. It's a continuous process and goes on even when you are not actively working toward it. So, make it HABITUAL and HABITABLE. Let's take cues for 'personality building' from the morning schedule itself:

- Get up on time when your alarm rings. After your daily routine, have breakfast by following small table etiquettes; have your briefcase and laptop bag arranged the night before, and ensure your clothes and shoes are ready. This will result in a hassle-free morning. Without a doubt, it will be a blissful experience for you and your family, who will always appreciate you for valuing your time.

Reach your office on time. After formal greetings with your colleagues and subordinate staff, get to your chair. Declutter your table and organise yourself for the day's work. We all know, "A cluttered mind is a devil's workshop."

- "Organising yourself is a very important part of your personality."
- Dispense the work and set deadlines. This can be done in the stand-up meeting at the start of the day.
- The people in your 'good books' should be diligent, dependable, and trustworthy. You may rely on them to ease out your work.

- Your personality will help you build these close-knit connections.
- Have an authoritative attitude or disposition. At the same time, show concern for your subordinates and initiate welfare steps for them. This will help your personality grow tall.
- Show promptness when taking accountability if you go wrong somewhere. Discuss the issue with colleagues or seniors to mitigate the problem rather than continuing with wrongdoings to satisfy your ego.
- Have an open, growth-oriented mindset. Be open to suggestions, even from your juniors. You can even reward your juniors to keep a healthy environment in the workplace and also develop a competitive spirit among all subordinates.
- Be a passionate learner, even when you are the CEO of your company. This is in the interest of your growth as well as your company's growth.
- Whenever you encounter a problem, try to approach your boss with one or two solutions rather than complaining about the difficulties and lacunae.
- A good leader or a person with a great personality is often judged by the effectiveness of their speech. So, be balanced in your speech and have a lot of connectivity with the listeners.
- A good personality is also reflected when the person is a careful listener and interrupts only when necessary.
- A powerful personality arises when it is genuine and not copied from anyone else, as well as when one is consistent, law-abiding, futuristic, and adaptable to new challenges.

During all this discussion, you may have thought that we have diverted from the topic of how to build one's personality. But if you study all these points deeply, it will make you a likeable, dependable, and respected person among people, which is all the result of your versatile personality.

ACTIVITY 3

My Roadmap to 'Carve a Niche'

1. My ways to create a good first impression are.........
....
....
....
....
....

2. My newly adopted ways to create a good first impression are...
....
....
....
....
....
....

3. I owe a great personality as I am...........................
....
....
....
....
....
....

4. Now, my personality has rebounded on the other side of the table as I adopted ....
....
....
....
....
....
....
....

Chapter Four
Manners And Etiquette

GOOD MANNERS AND ETIQUETTE AT WORKPLACE

"Let's not confuse traditional behaviours with good manners. The definition of etiquette is gender-neutral. It simply means we strive at all times to ensure a person in our company feels at ease."

- Lynn Coady

Etiquette is an extension of a good personality, which means that a person with good social and moral etiquette is bound to be the beholder of an impressive personality. It is a part and parcel of a great personality. We have been taught about basic etiquette and manners from the very beginning of our lives, and some phrases such as 'Thank you.' 'Please.' 'Sorry.' and 'Excuse me' have become intrinsic to us since then, and the list is endless.

But what kind of behaviour is expected of us as adults, especially when we are in the workplace? Let's learn some of these behavioural outcomes through real-life situations and try to get convinced, connected, and enlightened by them.

SITUATION 1

Suppose you have to meet your boss urgently, but there is a long queue of visitors waiting to meet him.

Etiquette you should follow:

You should either send a slip with your name and the 'purpose of your meeting' to your boss through the PA or peon or wait patiently for your turn if your work is not at immediate risk.

What should you avoid?

You should avoid peeping through the door repeatedly and trying to show your face. Under no circumstances should you create any ruckus, however important your work may be.

Worst-case scenario:

You can hand over your duties to any responsible colleague of yours and submit an application for leave at the reception, clearly mentioning the urgency that required your departure.

SITUATION 2

What do you do if you arrive a little late to the office, and your boss has already arrived, and you come face-to-face with him?

Etiquette you should follow:

In such a case, an honest answer is the best course of action. You can first apologise for being late and then explain the reason, whether you got stuck in traffic, someone was sick at home, you missed the bus/metro by a few minutes, or you worked late the previous night to meet a deadline.

What should you avoid?

Avoid giving reasons like 'I didn't hear the alarm.' 'I slept late at night, so I got up late.' or 'I went for a movie or dinner, so I got up late in the morning.'

Worst-case scenario:

If you were late for some personal reason, like sleeplessness due to work pressure, power breakdown, or no water supply in the taps, then you should tell your boss that you're unwell and need some rest, and you have come to apply for a day off.

SITUATION 3

What do you do if you are in an urgent meeting with important clients and your boss calls you in the midst of it?

Etiquette you should follow:

Very politely, you can excuse yourself from the meeting for a moment and step outside to speak to your boss on the intercom, explaining the urgency of the situation.

What should you avoid?

Don't shrug off the messenger or overlook the message. Also, avoid telling the messenger, "Tell the boss that I am busy in a meeting.".

Worst-case scenario:

There is no third option in this case. You must excuse yourself briefly and talk to your boss on the intercom. However, it is not necessary to meet the boss in person in this situation.

Learning how to deal with such situations will prepare you for any untoward or unforeseen events. Taking cues from the above common situations and how to deal with them in your office will automatically equip your mind with the wisdom and grit to face any challenge confidently.

SOME RULES OF ETIQUETTE

"Treat others as you would want to be treated by them."

- Anonymous

"Etiquette means behaving yourself a little better than is absolutely essential."

- Will Cuppy

Manners, morals, and values are the things that money can't buy, but good intent, adaptability, and practice are certain factors that can aid you in cultivating them—at absolutely no cost.

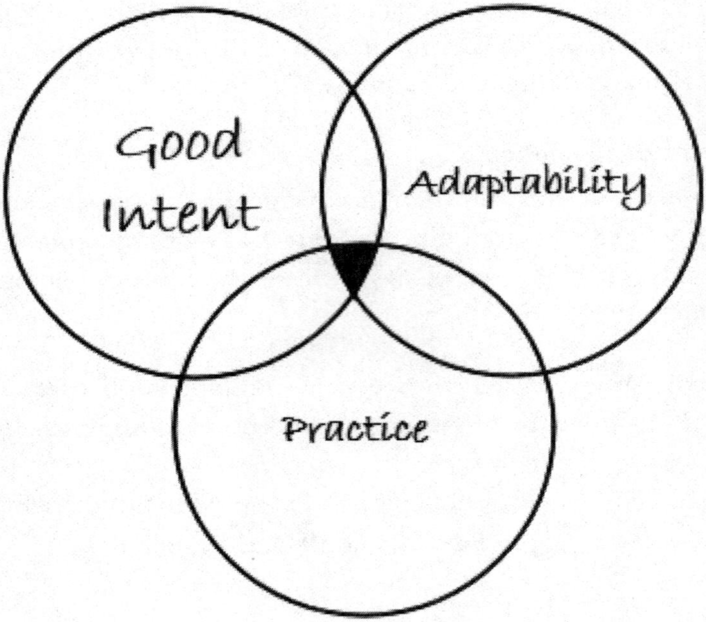

Shaded portion denotes Manners, Morals and Values

Let's take some examples to understand the rules of etiquette:

Example 1:

Imagine a student not understanding a concept or not having done his homework. The teacher begins shouting and even raises a stick to punish the child. This behaviour is in no way acceptable. So, what's the rule that follows?

Rule 1: Be polite; never be rude or harsh to a child or an adult. Instead, use mild, eclectic methods to help a child or an adult improve. From this example, we can also derive another rule:

Rule 2: One must watch their volume or pitch while talking to a child or an adult.

Example 2:

Imagine a teacher trying to counsel a child by saying, "If you don't mend your ways, I'll lock you up in the washroom," or "If you don't wear a neat and tidy uniform, you will be called out by 'names' by your fellow students."

Such methods of counselling are unacceptable. Instead, the teacher should find positive ways to reform the child.

Rule 3: Avoid negative remarks.

From this example, another rule follows:

Rule 4: One must think before carrying out any act.

Example 3:

Suppose, in an office, the boss frequently snubs a junior and uses foul language in front of the staff over petty issues.

This kind of behaviour not only demoralises the junior but also causes them to be insulted in front of everyone.

Rule 5: We should be respectful towards others.
There are many other ways by which you can counsel your junior, such as talking to them in private.

From this example, another rule follows:

Rule 6: One must choose their words very wisely and should never be abusive.

Example 4:

Suppose a colleague of yours is not very innovative, smart, or messy at work. How would you react to them in front of others or even the boss while having a general conversation? The expected behaviour is to talk positively about them. Never talk ill of them, no matter how dull they seem. Their work will be assessed and reflected in their performance review. So, the next rule of etiquette is:

Rule 7: Speak highly of others; be helpful, friendly, and courteous.

Example 5:

Suppose a person in your office is always complaining, cribbing, or clamouring about low wages, long hours of duty, no perks, no bonuses, and so on. How should you respond?

It's okay to say you feel underpaid, but it's not appropriate to keep ranting about it. There are professional ways to raise such issues and get them resolved. Also, there is no point in crying over it continuously; if it were unbearable, then you would have left the office. So, the rule of etiquette that follows is:

Rule 8: One should be grateful and appreciative of their workplace and to God, as it is the source of their livelihood.

Example 6:

Suppose you're at a workshop organised by your company, and the topic of the discussion does not concern you much. You soon feel bored and disinterested. How should you behave in such a situation?

The expected behaviour is to remain calm and composed. While you may overlook parts of the discussion, you should be in a position to respond wherever necessary to maintain a courteous disposition.

So, the rule of etiquette that follows is:

Rule 9: Always be courteous and responsive, whatever the situation.

From this example, another rule follows:

Rule 10: Be patient and practice active listening most of the time.

Rules of etiquette do not end here. With each new day and experience, you learn more and become a better version of yourself. Nobody can teach you or hand you a complete guide to etiquette; it's a lifestyle and work ethic that develops through your own experiences.

ACTIVITY 4

My Roadmap to 'Carve a Niche'

1. I have a good personality because I follow ....
   ....
   ....
   ....
   ....

2. My response in Situation 1 would be........................
   ....
   ....
   ....
   ....
   ....

3. My response in Situation 2 would be........................
   ....
   ....
   ....
   ....

4. My response in Situation 3 would be........................
   ....
   ....
   ....
   ....
   ....

5. I maintain a good balance between ...., ...,
   ....
   ....
   ....
   ....
   .... to strive to achieve or imbibe good manners, morals, and values.

Chapter Five
Hard Work

THERE IS NO SUBSTITUTE FOR HARD WORK

"Hard work is a prison sentence only if it does not have meaning. Once it does, it becomes the kind of thing that makes you grab your wife around the waist and dance a jig."

— Malcolm Gladwell

What is hard work? How do you define it? Whenever someone is doing a job, they try to do it in the best possible way to the best of their abilities. So, don't you think hard work is inevitable for any job and that we do it by default? This may be true for some, but for many, hard work feels like something imposed on them, something they are not prepared to do. We could, therefore, define 'hard work' as going the 'extra mile' to win any race. This 'extra mile' can be in the form of breaking several records while winning a race or accomplishing a task. Clearly, hard work is not easy, and yet to excel at the workplace demands that you outperform yourself.

To go the extra mile, you must constantly push yourself, challenge your own capabilities, and remain unsatisfied until you achieve the desired results.

When you have a 'burning ache.' it will drive your potential through hard work to the aplomb.

Now that we know that hard work does not come by default, we must strive to go the extra mile to invite it. Let's find out some of the ways by which we can motivate ourselves to do hard work.

1. Inbuilt Motivation:

Some people are born hardworking, and with the slightest encouragement, they feel positive and motivated. For them, work is either a form of worship or their appetite. These people require very little prompting and are always ready to put in extra hours to enhance the quality of their work. They just need to manage their work smartly.

2. Rewards or Bonuses:

When a company formulates certain stages or milestones to achieve, after which employees are appreciated or well rewarded, this acts as a great motivator for them. It fills them with encouragement to work hard to achieve the target or milestone.

3. Love for the Workplace:

When you love the job that you do or aspire to stay there for the long term, you will automatically remain motivated. In such a scenario, you will naturally try to 'carve a niche' at your workplace and will work hard to secure your place there and even potentially lead it one day.

4. Follow Your Idol:

Everyone has an idol whom they follow in life. They could be anyone: your parents, teacher, boss, celebrity, scientist, entrepreneur, or anyone who has left an indelible mark or has had an impact on your life. In a way, you are inspired by them and want to emulate them in your life. This drives you to work hard towards your goals.

5. Personal Needs:

When you recognise your potential and the right acumen for the desired position in life, you feel motivated to work hard to achieve that position.

6. Financial Needs:

Financial pressure is a powerful motivator. If you are driven in life to earn money to support your family financially, then you push yourself to work hard and achieve the stability that you desire. This is one of the most common factors behind people working hard across the globe.

7. Social Needs:

One would be highly motivated to work hard when they want not only social recognition but also a respected position in society.

> Regardless of the motivation behind working hard, it is clear that hard work and an aspiration to 'carve a niche' are directly connected. Only by working hard will you be able to establish your desired place in society.

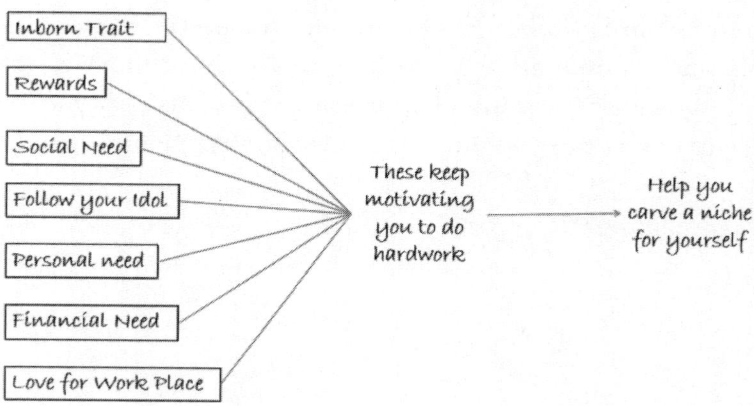

SET GOALS FOR YOURSELF

"Setting goals is the first step in turning
the invisible into the visible."

- Tony Robbins

Once the zeal for hard work has set in, the next step is to discipline or organise yourself by setting goals as per the nature of your work and the requirements of your company. If you do not set goals for yourself, you are likely to get into a whirlpool of work where you are directionless and overwhelmed. So, planning is absolutely essential to achieve a goal. You should have clear and well-defined thoughts about your work. There should be mental preparation about how to approach a particular task and how to plan it to achieve the desired results.

If your goals are properly set, you're halfway there. If your planning is not proper or fails, replace it with another plan after conducting thorough research, but don't change your goals after the initial failure. You set goals because they are important to you and, therefore, should be prioritised.

HOW TO TREAT GOALS?

One common question that comes to mind is, "How should we treat our goals, and how should we proceed toward them after establishing them to complete our work?"

Let me share an example from my own experience for further clarification:

As a coordinator in my school, I was often assigned deadlines, such as submitting question papers for upcoming exams, monthly planners, summer holiday homework, teachers' appraisals, and so on. The deadlines seemed never-ending, similar to goals.

Let's take GOAL 1/TASK 1 for example:

Submission of question papers for the upcoming scheduled exam

How should I go about doing this task? Where do I begin? How do I accomplish the task by the given deadline? How should I achieve this goal? How should I execute a task? So many questions immediately popped up the moment the task was given.

The answer to all these questions was simple; I would have to plan it out meticulously so that everything goes smoothly, from the collection of question papers from teachers to their typing, arranging them into sets by class and subject for different days on which the exams of different subjects would be conducted. Although the task was simple, when put in one sentence, it had multiple steps.

> From this example, you must understand that to achieve any goal (like here, the submission of the question papers), the task has to be divided into various "steps."

Let's break it down into simple steps to achieve this TASK 1 or say GOAL 1:

- **Step 1:** Inform the teachers in advance to complete the syllabus to be covered in the exam well in time.
- **Step 2:** Delegate a deadline to each subject teacher for submitting the question papers.
- **Step 3:** Give reminders to each subject teacher to ensure they submit on time.
- **Step 4:** Go through each paper and make corrections as needed, either by yourself or in consultation with the subject teacher (vetting of the question paper).
- **Step 5:** Incorporate the corrections/changes made in the question paper.
- **Step 6:** Send the corrected final question papers for photocopying.
- **Step 7:** Make sets subject-wise and class-wise according to the scheduled exam.

> So, it becomes clear that any seemingly simple task also requires careful planning and step-by-step execution to achieve the desired goal or target.

The above example represents a "short-term goal." Similarly, you can also deal with "long-term goals" with proper planning, structuring, dividing into steps, and then taking 'action.' Short-term goals at the workplace may be your day-to-day tasks. However, long-term goals are often related to career growth. These could vary from person to person, such as getting a promotion, receiving a hike in salary, developing interpersonal relations, improving communication skills, upgrading academic skills, and so on, to 'carve a niche' in your workplace.

Whatever your long-term goals may be, they can be achieved only after achieving the short-term goals.

WHAT SHOULD THE GOALS BE LIKE?

"Knowing is not enough; we must apply.
Willing is not enough; we must do."
- Johann Wolfgang Von Goethe

So, whether you talk about your short-term goals or your long-term goals, you should ensure that these goals are doable or workable. They should be realistic and relevant. They should be time-bound. Each goal should be discreet or definable.

But what do we exactly mean by all of these terms? Let's use some tasks (short-term or long-term) to understand them clearly.

- **The goal should be 'Doable:'**

Set a goal that is doable, workable, and achievable. Never set a goal that is nearly impossible and is beyond your reach.

For example, in task 1, avoid telling the teachers that you'll get the question papers typed for them or that they can submit handwritten papers. This could become a tedious goal to achieve because it may become unachievable over time if it becomes a regular practice with teachers.

- **The goal should be Realistic:**

This means that the goal should be practical and not idealistic.

For example, in task 1, it is realistic to ensure that teachers should only include the portion that is completed or will be completed by the time of the exams, accounting for some revision classes.

- **The goal should be Discreet/Definable:**

This means that the goal fixed by you should be clear in your mind, and you should be able to define it or express it clearly.

- **The goal should be Relevant:**

This means that your goal should have relevance to what you have planned to do. Don't set a 'vague' goal.

For example, in task 1, your goal is to collect question papers and make sets for the scheduled exam. With this specific goal, don't mix in other goals, such as whether the syllabus has been completed in all classes or not. So, don't mix two goals; rather, strive to achieve each goal separately.

- **The goal should be Time-bound:**

This means that you should be able to achieve your goal within the timeframe you set. The achievement of the target/goal can't continue to linger.

With this in mind, we can frame an 'Acronym' for 'what the goals should be like' based on the above keywords. They can be referred to as DRDRT Goals.

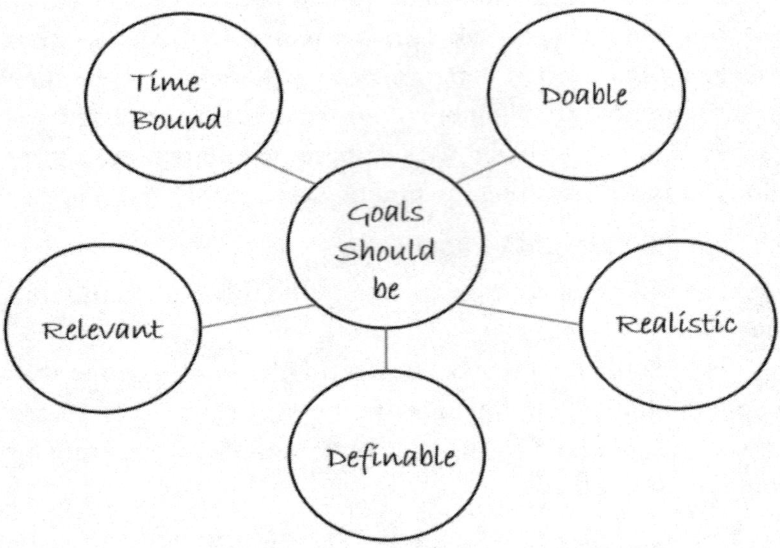

ACTIVITY 5

My Roadmap to 'Carve a Niche'

1. I am motivated to work the extra mile as I..................
....
....
....
....
....
....
....

2. I set 'short-term goals' so that I..............................
....
....
....
....
....
....

3. My 'long-term goals' are..
....
....
....
....
....

4. I set my goals and ensure that they are..................
...., ...
....
........, ...
..................., ...
................................, ...
....
....

Chapter Six
Professional Attitude

YOUR GUTS CAN MOVE MOUNTAINS

"True champions aren't always the ones that win,
but those with the most guts."

- Mia Hamm

"It takes knowledge to know something.
It takes guts to do what you know."

- Pete Wentz

"Guts win more games than ability."

- Robert Zuppke

One must maintain a 'professional attitude' in the workplace. By this, we mean that while at work, you should approach tasks, set goals, and make decisions in favour of the company, employees, society, and all immediate factors contributing to the company's interests without being swayed by whims or emotional biases. This doesn't mean that one has to become a tyrant, cold-hearted, or audacious while making decisions in a professional capacity. However, decisions should be well-considered and strike a good balance of honesty, capability, integrity, and the welfare of stakeholders.

So, having 'guts' is one of the positive aspects of possessing a professional attitude.

How can a person with guts be a resourceful and promising choice for any company, organization, or institute?

The answer is simple:

> Guts can trigger innovations that will always inspire subordinates to think 'outside the box' and give their best.

A person with guts is bold and courageous and always takes the initiative in making sound decisions for the company, striving to implement them promptly. Such individuals take calculated risks and know how to manage them. They also prove to be good leaders and individuals of substance. They possess excellent managerial skills while delivering better and quicker results for their companies. These individuals consistently initiate change, and with their strong willpower, they bring transformations at the grassroots level.

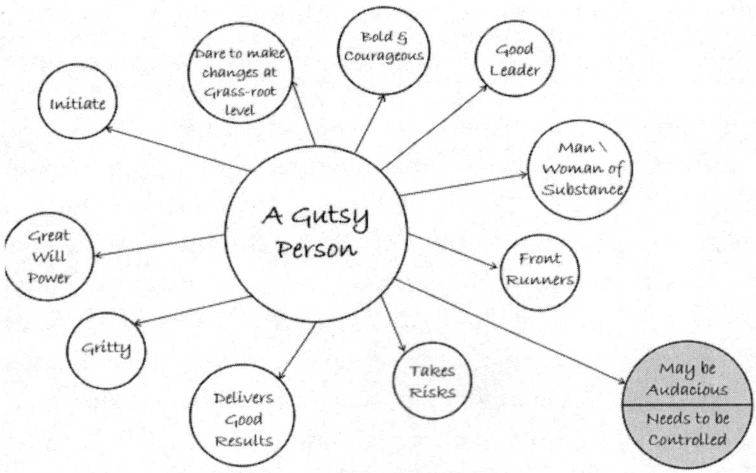

Now that we have seen so many positive qualities of a gutsy person, there are also certain 'cautionary signs' that depict or warn us of the potential downsides of such an audacious character. This needs to be managed by the person, or it might lead to their downfall.

We need to conclude that an amalgamation of 'guts' and 'abilities' creates the 'ideal managerial combination.'

It is important to mention that guts are innate, but they can certainly be cultivated with wisdom, training, and practice.

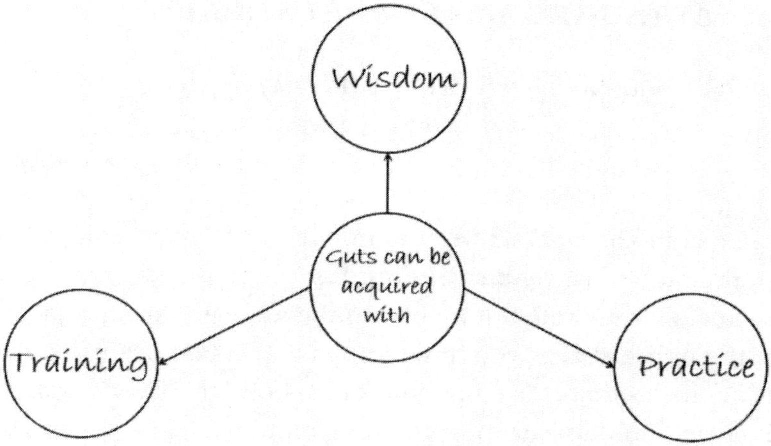
Wisdom
Guts can be acquired with
Training
Practice

ATTAINING LEADERSHIP QUALITIES

"A leader is one who knows the way, goes the way, and shows the way."

- John Maxwell

To excel in the workplace, it is important to possess that X factor known as 'leadership quality.' It helps you not only to excel in your role but also to make an everlasting impact on the organisation you're working in. Leaders are not only those in national or international politics. Every small or large company or organisation requires leaders to run effectively and smoothly. We know very well that from the recruitment pool of aspirants, only a few rise to leadership positions, taking titles such as manager, CEO, COO, CFO, HOD, Chief, Coordinator, Principal, Commissioner, and so on. So, what's that X factor that all these leaders possess? Why are they the chosen ones? How did they manage to reach such heights? How did they surpass their colleagues?

The answer is that they possess leadership qualities.

So, what are these qualities that have led to such a rise over others?

At this point, you would all agree with me on one common quality that all of them possess, which is their ability to 'carve a niche' in their organisation successfully.

The question that immediately comes to mind is, what are those qualities that helped them 'carve a niche' to lead their organisation successfully?

Let's shed some light on these leadership qualities. One can be a good leader by birth, but mostly, leadership qualities are attained through self-appraisal over time. A person may be very good at bossing others by nature, but if he's not properly educated or doesn't have deep knowledge in his field, he may not be regarded as a leader in the true sense.

Likewise, a leader needs to possess many other qualities that will help him outshine others.

Some of these leadership qualities that resonate with me are as follows:

- **Appropriately Qualified:**

A leader should have the right education in their field with proper merits and credentials. A thorough knowledge of one's field instills confidence in their work.

- **Good Communication Skills:**

A leader should have clarity of thoughts and ideas and should be able to articulate them effectively. The ideas and thoughts delivered should be rational, logical, impactful, pertinent, and inclusive.

- **Team Spirit/Advocacy for Collaboration:**

A leader should foster a collaborative attitude. They are not just a manager but also a philosopher and guide for the team. They should delegate work, set deadlines, solicit feedback, and help the team improve consistently to make a profound impact on the organisation. A true leader should encourage teamwork and promote inclusivity rather than self-promotion.

- **Caring and Good Interpersonal Relations:**

A leader can engage with subordinates to get to know them personally, which can help address professional issues such as salary, promotions, workload, office hours, and transfers. This should be done for the welfare of the subordinates and in the interest of the company.

- **Self-Motivated:**

A leader should be well-acquainted with contemporary changes in their field and should be enthusiastic about adopting and incorporating those changes to enhance both themselves and the company, reflecting on growth.

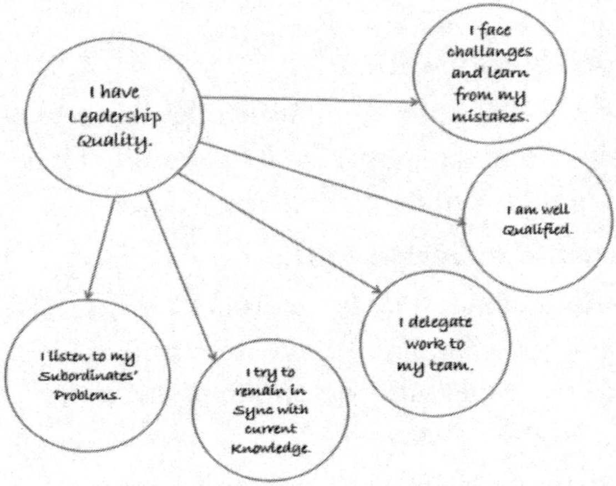
I have Leadership Quality.
I face challanges and learn from my mistakes.
I am well Qualified.
I delegate work to my team.
I listen to my Subordinates' Problems.
I try to remain in Sync with current Knowledge.

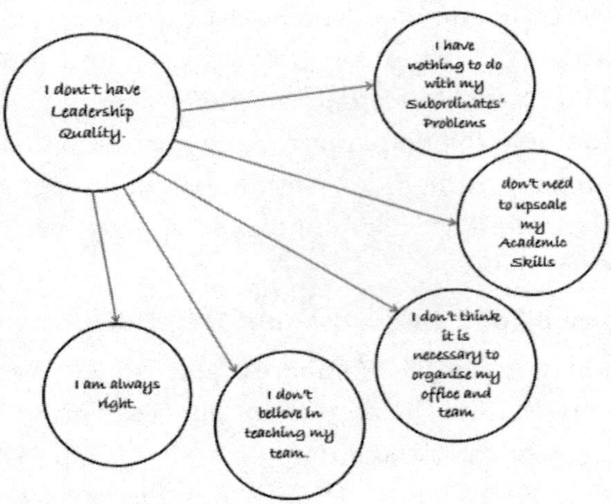
I don't have Leadership Quality.
I have nothing to do with my Subordinates' Problems
don't need to upscale my Academic Skills
I don't think it is necessary to organise my office and team
I am always right.
I don't believe in teaching my team.

- **Well-Organised:**

A leader should structure a department to ensure smoother and easier functioning right from the grassroots level.

- **Role Model for Others:**

The team looks up to their leader in every way. A leader should project an ethical, sincere, accountable, and morally good image to inspire their team.

- **Resilient:**

A leader should be resilient in times of challenges. Their 'inner self' should push them to learn from mistakes and stand tall and strong.

RESPECT FOR THE BOSS EARNS YOU RESPECT

"Your leadership and vision made you a great boss, but your integrity, respect, and compassion make you a great person."

- www.idlehearts.com

It's a fundamental aspect of a 'professional attitude' to respect your boss, as it not only earns you respect but also enhances your self-esteem, pride, and honour, enabling you to maintain a good and healthy relationship with them. This attitude is essential and symbolises a commendable professional demeanour. It's important to be congenial, respectful, positive, and productive with your boss.

The boss judges you on several parameters related to respect, some of which I have listed here:

- Your 'well-disciplined' demeanour in front of them.
- Your 'manner of speaking' should be respectful and honest.
- Your 'body language' should be sincere and demonstrate professionalism.
- Your communication should be specific, concise, and self-explanatory.
- Refrain from personal conversations unless it genuinely requires the boss's intervention.
- Value your boss's directives and intervene only when you have a valid point.
- Remember to be 'well-dressed,' adhering to the dress code if applicable.

- Show alertness and maintain a calm demeanour.
- Above all, your 'courteous behaviour' leaves a lasting impression on your boss.

Overall, maintaining a calm and composed mind while upholding your honour and dignity, alongside the highest standards of discipline and courtesy in front of your boss, will earn you a permanent place in their thoughts.

CAN SYCOPHANCY HELP ME CREATE MY NICHE?

Here, I must clarify that 'appeasement or sycophancy' will not help you secure a permanent or top-tier position in your company. These so-called negative attributes may work to a certain extent. They might help you develop a relationship with your boss faster than others, or they may even fetch you short-term gains like quick recognition, proximity to your boss, or a few other favours.

> However, the true, authentic essence of your professional life can only be achieved by following a dedicated, honest, and respectful path of progression amalgamated with your knowledge and experience.

Sycophancy might get you noticed immediately, but in the long run, only dedication to your work will pay off. You may become likeable or lovable momentarily, but as soon as the boss realises that you are merely an 'empty vessel making much noise,' you'll be dismissed from their mind. A boss will always welcome a person who brings solutions to problems along with innovative ideas and new knowledge. A sycophant lacking these traits will only serve as a temporary diversion or a tool for the boss.

The dedicated individual will earn the boss's genuine attention and reliance as they are the 'pillar' of any organisation.

Sycophancy might seem effective, but the foundation of success is always built on hard work and dedication. Therefore, sycophancy is short-lived and cannot secure your place or niche in the organisation.

Nothing better can be said about a sycophant than this: "How can he (today's writer) be honoured when he does not honour himself; when he loses himself in the crowd; when he is no longer the lawgiver, but the sycophant, ducking to the giddy opinion of a reckless public." - Ralph Waldo Emerson

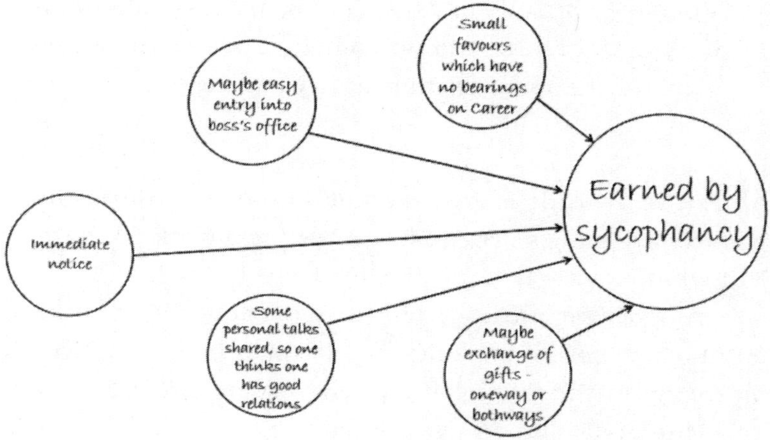

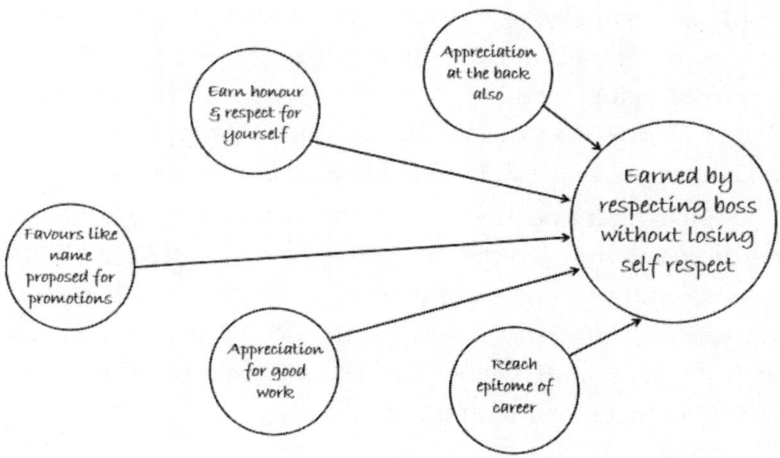

POSITIVE ATTITUDE IS THE BACKBONE OF ANY SUCCESS

"A positive attitude causes a chain reaction of positive thoughts, events, and outcomes. It is a catalyst and sparks extraordinary results."

- Wade Boggs

A positive attitude is key to professionalism. Maintaining a positive attitude is crucial for achieving a work-life balance. But what exactly is a positive attitude?

A positive attitude is displayed when you show enthusiasm for your work; when you bring a positive vibe or energy to the workplace, when you are productive while believing in a collaborative mindset.

You demonstrate positivity in your actions when you adopt an inclusive approach that works in conjunction with your subordinates, taking adequate steps to ensure their well-being. You set a positive tone in the workplace when you prioritise the welfare of your subordinates, show consideration, and exhibit empathy towards them.

You exhibit a positive attitude when you actively promote the professional growth of your subordinates, perhaps by facilitating regular workshops and training programs. You embody positivity when, in the face of challenges, you motivate your staff by helping them improve rather than criticising them for their failures.

So, positivity in the workplace revolves around a collective, coherent, and abundant thought process where everyone's problems or shortcomings are acknowledged. We persistently strive to lead by example, taking greater responsibility for connecting, correlating, and uplifting everyone around us with positive thoughts and actions.

Which route should I take to be congenial in my workplace, or in other words, to show positive action?

Write 'P' for the positive route in the following cases:

	Situation		Route (A/B)
1	I am not at Par academically with my collegues, so I feel frustrated. My boss told me to get early leave sanctioned and join some part time refresher course.	(A)	I should leave office a little early everyday to join the part time course to upgrade my skills.
		(B)	I should take a long leave & Join a full time regular course and if leave is not sanctioned, I should turn away the job.
2	I feel uneasy, tired, perplexed when I am loaded with work. My Boss suggested me to join yoga and meditation classes held in office during break time.	(A)	I should join Yoga and meditation classes in office break time and relax myself a bit.
		(B)	I should join Yoga and meditation classes on weekends when i am at Home.
3	I am gullible to office politics and feel depressed often. Although my boss is very positive and appreciates me often.	(A)	I should talk to my boss regarding my uneasiness in the current office and should request for a transfer to a different section.
		(B)	I should leave the job and keep myself away from the muck and look for another job.

Through these examples or situations, we can clearly see that with a positive attitude, we learn to face challenges. We become more resilient, and we attune ourselves to the world.

There are three MAGIC WORDS to remain positive, irrespective of how harsh the situation is.

Any guesses?

Yes, we know them! They are around us all the time, but we don't grasp them because MAYBE WE'RE NOT POSITIVE ENOUGH.

These 'magic words' are:

- Never lose COURAGE,
- Always give it another TRY, and
- Demonstrate RESILIENCE.

ACTIVITY 6

My Roadmap to 'Carve a Niche'

1. I show a professional attitude in my workplace as I am fairly 'gutsy' because of my qualities such as......
....
....
....
....

2. I show a professional attitude in my workplace as I possess 'leadership qualities' such as....................
....
....
....

3. I show a professional attitude in my workplace as I 'respect my boss' by...
....
....
....

4. I show a professional attitude by 'not adopting sycophancy' because it ....
....
....
....
....

5. I show a professional attitude by keeping a 'positive attitude' in the workplace by..................................
....
....
....
....

Chapter Seven
Imbibing Qualities

A RECEPTIVE MIND PAYS OFF

"Being receptive, being able to listen openly and well,
is a skill for creative problem-solving."

- Paul A. Kaufman

If you're seeking to build upon professional attitudes (as you already possess some professional attitudes and now want to acquire or enhance the existing ones with the knowledge you gained in the previous chapter), here are a few crucial characteristics that a manager, new entrant, or recruit should possess.

> These characteristics form the basis on which 'professional attitudes' can be built.We can enumerate these characteristics as having a receptive mind, being a careful listener, being good at documenting, being an enthusiastic learner, and possessing cooperative manners.

A lot has been said about the ''pros' of having a receptive mind.

Let's understand the advantages by first recognising the 'cons' of having an "unreceptive mind."

An unreceptive mind is not open to suggestions or new ideas.

- An unreceptive mind always believes it is right.
- An unreceptive mind tends to be complacent.
- An unreceptive mind will impose its beliefs everywhere, all the time.
- An unreceptive mind is often overconfident and proud.
- An unreceptive mind may lack a progressive vision.

- An unreceptive mind will be self-opinionated and unable to bring in new techniques for upgrading the company.
- An unreceptive mind clings to old clichés and lacks creativity.

Here, I would like to highlight that a good leader or a person with leadership qualities is someone who has a 'receptive mind.'

So, what exactly does one gain by having a 'receptive mind?'

How does a receptive mind make one a good leader?

These questions are easy to answer once you understand the 'cons' of an unreceptive mind.

Renowned poet William Wordsworth once said, "The child is the father of man," meaning the habits or personality of a person are shaped by their behaviour and conduct during childhood. Thus, a person is likely to be unreceptive if they have exhibited such tendencies since childhood.

However, even if a person is unreceptive, they can improve once they recognise that their growth is hindered by this trait. After all, a mature and responsible mind knows what is good and what is detrimental to their progress. Therefore, a 'receptive mind' is one of the essential criteria for developing a 'professional attitude.'

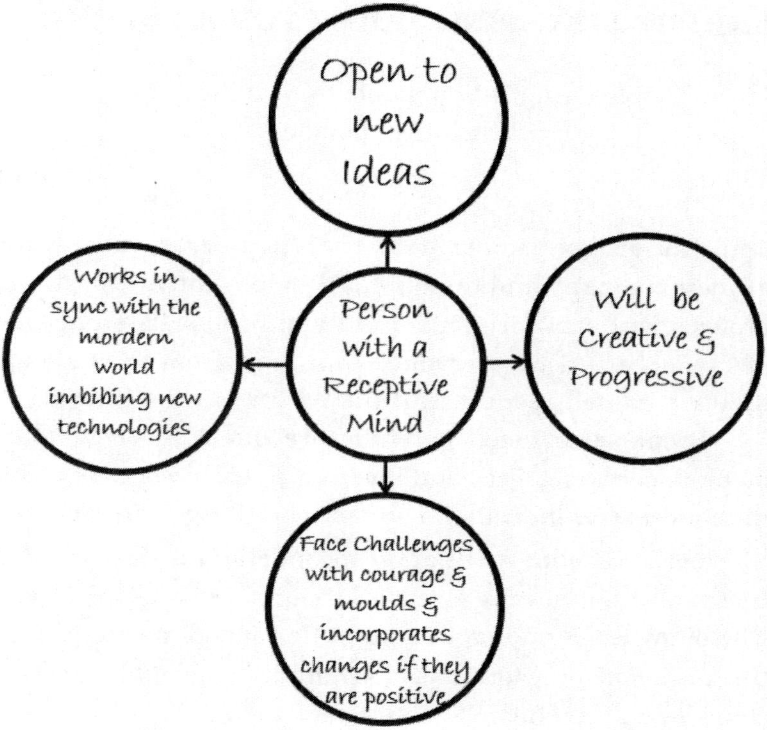
Open to new Ideas
Works in sync with the mordern world imbibing new technologies
Person with a Receptive Mind
Will be Creative & Progressive
Face Challenges with courage & moulds & incorporates changes if they are positive

ARDENT LISTENING TAKES YOU A LONG WAY

"Listening is being able to be changed by the other person."

- Alan Alda

Being an ardent listener truly enables a person to advance in their company and undoubtedly helps cultivate a 'strong' professional attitude. This quality of ardent listening may not be accepted by everyone, as it may seem to challenge their ego or self-respect. But the reality is very different.

People who listen carefully are often observed to be more sincere, engaged, and invested in their work. It is said that successful individuals do more listening than talking.

Let's consider a situation to understand this better. A friend of mine always acted as though he was overflowing with knowledge and would skip after-school meetings with the principal or coordinator, claiming he would later ask someone to brief him.

Now, in such a situation, what exactly did that friend miss? Did he miss something important, or did he compensate for the loss by asking a colleague for superficial details?

Let's analyse this situation.

Yes, certainly, that person missed a lot! Let's enumerate.

- He doesn't know how much emphasis was placed on certain points in the meeting.
- He doesn't understand the tone and tenor of the supervisor during the meeting.
- He won't grasp which issues were most critical during the discussion and what the supervisor's final decisions were.

- He won't understand the choices/options suggested by the supervisor for solving particular problems.
- He would miss the opportunity to have his name included or excluded from a specific task.

On the whole, he would have missed the overall 'feel' of the meeting or discussion and would be left with just the 'gist' of it.

By now, you would agree with me that listening is extremely important.

I'll shed some light on the advantages of being an ardent listener:

- You can grasp, absorb, and adapt to the environment of the company while developing cordial interpersonal relationships with your colleagues and seniors.
- You gain exposure through listening, which provides you a good opportunity to improve yourself and hone your skills.
- You are seen as a sincere, hard-working, and dependable person, which keeps you in the good books of your supervisor.
- When you attend numerous workshops, seminars, discussions, etc., you certainly grow and flourish, which will help you in your future career, where you may be elevated to senior ranks.
- If you're already complacent about your knowledge and potential, you'll hardly learn anything new, putting a full stop to your personal and professional growth.
- Only an ardent listener can think in broader perspectives for the company as they continuously grow in terms

of technology, new courses of study, staff development, advocating new roadmaps for the company, and showcasing it on a global platform.

In summary, the progress of the company will be directly proportional to the performance of ardent listeners. In turn, ardent listeners will have a direct impact on themselves, helping them to 'carve their niche' as they align with the interests of the company with both mind and heart.

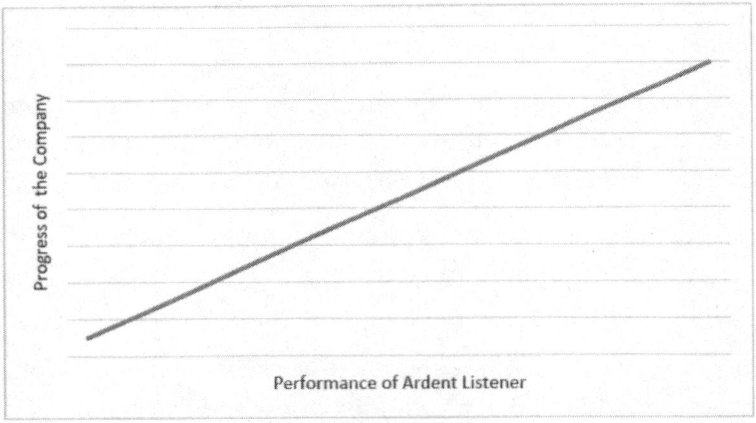

DOCUMENTATION IS A NECESSARY EVIL

"A little evil is often necessary for obtaining a great good."

- Voltaire

"Documenting is more than staying organised or writing down what will be or was taught. Documenting is part of the learning process."

- Silvia Tolisano

"Documentation is not about what we do, but what we are searching for."

- Carla Rinaldi

In our quest to build a 'Professional Attitude,' the next important aspect is documentation. What should one document? Everything important, such as what your supervisors said, documenting the orders they issued from time to time, recording minutes of meetings, noting what you learned in various workshops and seminars attended, documenting various guidelines issued by authorities, and recording feedback from yourself and others—in a way, practically documenting everything you observe in your workplace.

Under the heading 'Documentation,' we shall learn three things: What should we document? Why should we document? And how and where should we document?

One thing should be clear in your mind: documentation is mandatory, even though it may be cumbersome. We may not memorise the "Whats," "Whys," and "Hows" of documents, but we're always free to devise our methods according to our convenience and requirements. As has been said time and again, "Necessity is the mother of all inventions." Our quest for learning to document is simply limited to the understanding that documentation must be done daily or even hourly as per requirement, and that it serves as our greatest saviour when the need arises. Such is the power and role played by documentation in our office lives.

Let's shed some light on **WHAT SHOULD WE DOCUMENT**:

- Document the minutes of meetings, as they help you focus on upcoming targets, deadlines, and strategies for resolving issues.
- Document the various guidelines and policies of the company or institution for quick reference whenever you need clarification.
- Document any untoward incidents at your workplace for easy compliance whenever required.
- Document feedback from parents, clients, etc., to continually improve yourself and make changes in policies or incorporate new ones as necessary.
- Document various records of employees (even personal ones), inventories, and observation records by teachers/ authorities for any future compliance.

Document financial records such as fee statuses, other income sources, and expenditures to keep the financial status of the institution updated.

- Document anything new you learn from workshops or the Internet to provide valuable input, present models for the same, and be able to 'carve your niche' in your second family.'.

Once you know what we should document, our next pressing question is: **WHY SHOULD WE DOCUMENT?**

This question has been partly answered above, where we discussed what we should document. To further strengthen our understanding of 'documentation needs,' we should elaborate on the pertinent question: why should we document?

- We should document to keep reminding ourselves of the 'agenda for the day... week... month... year...' and so on.
- We should document them because these records help us achieve our goals, as the path to reaching those goals will be clearly defined in the document format.
- We will be able to meet the company's targets because we have documented the methods discussed in office meetings.
- Most importantly, documentation helps us continuously improve ourselves as we embrace the culture of our workplace through regular documenting and practising to our full capacity.
- Documentation provides evidence in any untoward or emergency situation.

I believe that through logical reasoning, you can think of many more reasons for answering the question: 'Why should we document?'

> Documentation is a significant practice, and it's essential for everyone to understand this from the moment they start a job. The human brain is a vast storage device but has limited memory, so we must transfer information from our minds to documented forms, whether on paper or digitally.

From the above discussion, it is clear that due to the limitations of human memory, one should document important information elsewhere. So, let's try to answer the question: **HOW & WHERE SHOULD WE DOCUMENT?**

Firstly, let's briefly talk about 'how we should document' to ensure that the information is easily accessible. Here are some good tips:

- Document in a manner that allows easy access to the pages you need. This can be done by putting 'flags,' 'labelling,' or marking the pages with headings, subheadings, and 'underlining' key sentences or keywords.
- Documents should be organised in proper 'files and folders' if stored on a computer. For handwritten documents, use separate diaries, notebooks, or file covers.
- Always mention the date, day, and time while documenting.
- Documentation should be in clear and understandable language. There is no need for flowery language, but avoid relying too heavily on shorthand.
- Sensitive data should be stored securely.
- Whether digital or handwritten, documents may need to be updated periodically to share the latest information with your subordinates or supervisors.

From the above, one can infer that documentation facilitates the transfer of information to the team, promoting collaboration, which is one of the crucial professional attitudes of a recruit or manager.

Now, WHERE SHOULD WE DOCUMENT?

We have partly answered this question above. Documentation can be easily and effectively done on a **COMPUTER** or as **HANDWRITTEN/TYPED** mediums.

In today's technology-driven world, where nothing works without machines, it is essential to know how to store data on a computer. One way is to create files and folders on a desktop or within the system.

Very briefly, I'll mention a few more methods to make it more informative and efficient. Documentation can be done and stored on:

- Notepad
- Digital platforms like Microsoft 365, Dropbox, and Notion.
- Project management software like Basecamp and Smartsheet.
- Shared drives include Google Drive, Microsoft OneDrive, Apple iCloud Drive, and Amazon Drive.

At the end of the day, it is 'learning to embrace the need for documentation' that will help you a million times indirectly and aid .'you in 'carving your niche.' Why indirectly? It is because if you're documenting regularly, you'll always be aware of the nuances of your project or office, making you ready to face questions promptly when necessary.

Your functioning will be much more organised and smooth.

- You will always be ahead of your time and your team.
- You will be well-informed about your current and future projects.
- You will have prompt answers and a visionary approach towards your goals.
- You will be better positioned to understand your responsibilities and accountabilities in your job sphere.
- You will be the most attentive, alert, and informed person at every meeting, seminar, conference, etc.

Don't you think these indirect attributes will have a direct impact on your path to 'carving a niche' for yourself?

NOTHING CAN STOP AN ENTHUSIASTIC LEARNER FROM GROWING

"In the realm of ideas, everything depends on enthusiasm... in the real world, all rests on perseverance."

- Johann Wolfgang Von Goethe

"A wise person knows that there is something to be learned from everyone."

- Anonymous

To be an enthusiastic or passionate learner, even after completing your studies, is a crucial factor in building a professional attitude.

You might think that with the completion of school and college, your quest for knowledge ends; but this is where you are mistaken.

Learning is an ongoing process that continues throughout life. As you pursue your career, the need to upgrade or update your knowledge becomes even more intense.

The reason is simple: when you're working, it becomes imperative to stay updated with the current advancements in your field, including developments in technology. But why is this necessary? Research is rapidly evolving across various fields, leading to the emergence of new learning methods. To keep in sync with changing methodologies and technologies, one needs to stay current to function smoothly and progressively.

How can you upgrade yourself while working?

- By enrolling in short-term academic courses in your field.
- By attending online or offline workshops and seminars.

- By regularly listening to field experts.
- By engaging in hands-on experiences.
- By keeping abreast of the latest technology through podcasts, technical journals, and other online resources.

Once you incorporate all these practices into your work schedule, they will become an integral part of your daily routine. The overall impact of such a change in your disposition will be significant, leading you toward the ultimate goal of 'carving a niche' for yourself in your workplace.

The passion or enthusiasm you cultivate by adopting these practices in your office routine will help you achieve your goals and targets within your company.

These practices will position you ahead of your peers, allowing you to grow rapidly with additional accomplishments.

On the other hand, what will be the outcome if you're not an enthusiastic learner?

- You will lag behind in your knowledge of your field, resulting in becoming overly dependent or professionally crippled.
- You will lose confidence in your abilities and shy away from challenges.
- Your promotions and perks will be adversely affected.
- You will miss opportunities to showcase your skills and prove your worth.

BE A CONGENIAL PERSON TO ALWAYS LEAD

"The best index to a person's character is how he treats people who can't do him any good and how he treats people who can't fight back."

- Abigal Van Buren

"Corporate culture matters. How management chooses to treat its people impacts everything for better or for worse."

- Simon Sinek

Being friendly, amiable, or congenial in your work environment helps you build interpersonal relationships and fosters a sense of ease. It's a trait that forms the foundation for leadership in your workplace. As we have discussed in previous chapters, leadership qualities are essential for cultivating a professional attitude.

Let's elaborate on what it means to be congenial in the workplace.

By being congenial, you automatically gain the following advantages:

- You become approachable to colleagues, subordinates, and supervisors.
- You learn more about your coworkers, their habits, temperament, nature, working styles, ethics, families, etc.
- With this knowledge, you can interact with them in a more articulate and authentic way.
- You become capable of dealing with them on a personal level, resulting in more impactful interactions.
- These traits contribute to developing healthy interpersonal relationships with colleagues and managers.

- By being congenial, you automatically become the most beloved and dependable person in your workplace.
- You earn the trust of others, making you highly regarded.
- You become the go-to person for everyone during difficult times, thereby gaining popularity.

These traits lead to a transformation of your image from an ordinary employee to a leading figure within the company. Such attributes are managerial traits (as we have previously discussed) and serve the interests of both the company and yourself.

A congenial person is also friendly with clients and other stakeholders, contributing to the growth of the company or institution by expanding the clientele.

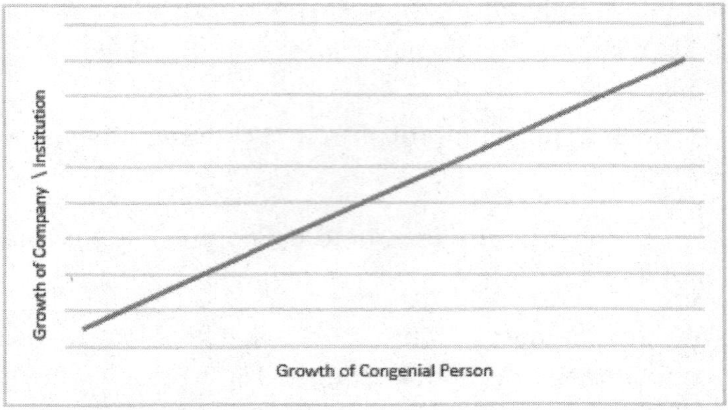

Congeniality is directly Proportional to the growth of the Company\ Institution

Congeniality is directly proportional to the growth of the company or institution.

There is another aspect to consider. Let's explore this comprehensively with some supporting statements.

A congenial person, in simple terms, is a friendly individual. Being friendly with colleagues doesn't mean that a congenial person has to please everyone through flattery or sycophancy or by offering monetary benefits, etc. It also doesn't mean that a congenial person must strive to satisfy everyone; failing to do so might lead to criticism from those who feel neglected.

A CONGENIAL PERSON DOESN'T HAVE TO BE A PEOPLE-PLEASER because, in the race to appease everyone, they may end up solving trivial disputes, which could interfere with their designated work.

> Congeniality is a trait that should come from within; you can develop it without compromising your work style, ethics, or originality. Being congenial is largely part of human nature, and you just need to work on it to cultivate it further.

ACTIVITY 7

My Roadmap to 'Carve a Niche'

1. I'm receptive, and that helps me to..........................
....
....
....

2. I'm an ardent listener because I ....
....
....
....

3. I document, and it helps me in ....
....
....
....

4. I'm an enthusiastic learner, and that helps me to
....
....
....
....

5. I'm a congenial person, and that helps me in developing... ....
....
....
....

6. I have imbibed qualities like...................................
....,...........................
....,...............
....,
...................................,..
.... which will help me develop a professional attitude.

Chapter Eight
Yes Man

IS A YES MAN A WEAK PERSON?

"You don't have to say yes to everything. You only need to learn to be open to the possibility."

- Leadership Lessons from Yes Man

"We can think we have nothing to offer. We can think we are not good enough. We are wrong."

- Leadership Lessons from Yes Man

Now that we have seen that to build a 'professional attitude,' we need to imbibe certain qualities such as having a receptive mind, being an ardent listener, developing documentation habits, being an enthusiastic learner, and being amiable, one question that inevitably comes to mind is, "Can we be true professionals only when we embody all the virtues of a true gentleman?"

The reason I mention a true gentleman here is that he is often seen as synonymous with a Yes Man.

A true gentleman is the apple of everyone's eye. He is rarely criticised and gains respect and authority through his goodness and circumspect personality, which has very few flaws. Thus, we can deduce from these characteristics that since such a gentleman receives almost no criticism, he resembles what we commonly refer to as a 'Yes Man' at work.

So, we can define a 'Yes Man' as a person who generally agrees with what his supervisors say.

We can also derive the following traits of a Yes Man:

- A Yes Man has no opponents or adversaries.
- A Yes Man is seen as a perfect human being.
- A Yes Man possesses all virtues.
- A Yes Man has little to no vices in the workplace.

All these arguments lead us to one significant conclusion:

"A true professional is a true gentleman who is also a Yes Man, reflected in his office etiquette, mannerisms, and respectfulness."

From the above discussion, we can also conclude that there is no harm in being a 'Yes Man' in professional life. A Yes Man is always welcomed in the manager's room. He is in good standing where the philosophy 'Respect Begets Respect' writes all chapters. This creates a relationship built on mutual understanding, much like how the banks of a river are always connected through the deep waters.

However, several questions arise: Is a Yes Man taken for granted? Does the viewpoint of a Yes Man carry any weight? Are the answers from a Yes Man already known to the manager, leading the manager to feel relaxed in his company?

Let me illustrate this with a real-life scenario:

A young man who graduated from one of the top tech colleges gets placed in one of the leading tech companies. He performs well and efficiently completes all tasks assigned to him ahead of deadlines. Since he obediently fulfils all the tasks per his manager's instructions, he is well-liked by the manager. However, because of his sincere nature, he becomes overburdened with work, as he never opposes or denies his manager's decisions. He even works beyond the stipulated hours to complete everything. Despite this extra burden, he could have easily procrastinated or made a genuine excuse, or he could have expressed his incapacity by saying that the task was too lengthy and complicated to finish on time. In other words, he could have easily stated his inability to meet the deadline while still showcasing his diligence in his work.

So, what I mean to say is that this young man is a Yes Man who never questions anything. Yet, such a Yes Man is often perceived as weak, foolhardy, or impractical.

> The fact is that being a Yes Man is not foolish; rather, it helps you to 'Carve your Niche.' Because a Yes Man works diligently and follows instructions, he quickly becomes a trusted and dependable person in the company. He is given more challenging tasks and more opportunities to prove himself. Supervisors rely on him so much that he effortlessly captures a key position within the company.

Such a person who is a Yes Man is not weak; however, he might overburden himself or exhaust himself to a greater degree. This must be managed by all means necessary.

Achieving this isn't too difficult if a person can maintain a good work model by restructuring their working style and rescheduling tasks to reduce the burden. At the same time, he can remain a Yes Man and lead a comfortable existence.

A YES MAN HAS GOALS DIFFERENT FROM OTHERS

So, can we say that it's good to be a Yes Man? Before answering this question, let's broadly reflect on the characteristics of a Yes Man:

Yes, a Yes Man has goals that differ from others. Let's enumerate how:

A Yes Man is committed to his work.

- A Yes Man values the people he interacts with.
- A Yes Man is trustworthy.
- A Yes Man is not distracted by the whims and fancies of others.
- A Yes Man exemplifies positive behaviour wherever he works.
- A Yes Man earns the trust of others because he is honest in his work, allowing him to gain favors, such as obtaining loans or shares in the company.
- A Yes Man has great contributions to offer to his company and, more broadly, to society.

HE OFFERS WORK ETHICS AND VALUES

Some traits of a Yes Man give him an edge over others in daily life:

- In life, a Yes Man opens doors to new opportunities for himself because he refrains from conflicts and embraces new ideas, challenges, and changes with open arms.
- Such a person readily accepts his duties and responsibilities. He pays his taxes on time and repays his loans punctually, leading banks to readily provide loans to such responsible individuals.
- He is dutiful and honest, thus excelling in every aspect of life.
- A Yes Man is well-organised. He tries his best and succeeds in maintaining a work-life balance.
- Because of his organisational skills, he rarely creates a mess at home. He understands situations and resolves them with utmost sincerity. He is more level-headed in life.

> If a person can maintain a good work-life balance, he has nearly reached the top of the flight of steps. In other words, such a person who is fulfiled at home will undoubtedly be the best contributor to their workplace and society.

From this discussion, we understand that an important 'virtue of life' is maintaining a work-life balance, which is the key to happiness in life. This essential virtue is well embodied by a Yes Man.

WITH DIFFERENT GOALS, A YES MAN EXCELS EVERYWHERE

Since a Yes Man is wholly committed to his work, he exudes an 'air of no-nonsense.' He is 'least bothered about the office politics' that may unfold or about management issues. He is 'sincerely working' to 'achieve his goals,' which are in the best interest of his company or institution. He won't pay any heed to ''office gossip.' Because a Yes Man is 'focused' on his objectives and work, he possesses the strength of iron.

It is his commitment to work and keeping a keen eye on his goals that enables him to face any harsh situation.

Only when a person has a 'solid foundation' (full of wisdom, commitment, honesty, and diligence) will they develop a 'tough exterior.' A Yes Man must be resilient because often, a true and honest Yes Man is undermined when someone cunningly finds fault in him to undermine him for some unfair reason. During such circumstances, the Yes Man must be careful and keep his emotions in check to avoid getting caught in the web of a manipulative individual. Wisdom and wit are essential in navigating troubled waters.

It's been quite a lecture thus far. Since we've discussed some traits of a Yes Man, let's play a 'chequered game' based on these traits.

Add all the numbers that align with you and that you agree with.

If your score is 187, you're a true Yes Man.

I Say Yes to 1 Friend's Invitation	I Say Yes to 2 Friend in need	I Say No to 3 Distressed Colleague	I Say No to 4 Outgoing Boss	I Say Yes to 5 colleague's Mother's Funeral
I Say No to 6 Lend money to Friend in need	I Say No to 7 Help in Cooking	I Say Yes to 8 Help my Children in studies	I Say Yes to 9 Cleaning Utensils	I Say No to 10 Helping maid financially
I Say Yes to 11 Gardening	I Say Yes to 12 Filing my returns	I Say No to 13 Being all people pleaser	I Say No to 14 Gossips	I Say Yes to 15 Office Politics
I Say No to 16 New Technology	I Say No to 17 Greetings in the morning	I Say Yes to 18 Leg Pulling	I Say Yes to 19 Back Biting	I Say No to 20 Being self-Centered
I Say Yes to 21 Mingling with Colleagues	I Say Yes to 22 Other's Suggestions	I Say No to 23 Honesty	I Say No to 24 Sycophancy	I Say Yes to 25 High Morals

Add all the numbers which have lines that relate to you or you agree with.
If your score is above 187, you are a true Yes-Man.

This game is purely my creation and has nothing to do with psychological assessments or tests.

'YES' MAKES THINGS COME ALIVE

"The big question is whether you are going to be able to say a hearty yes to your adventure."

- Joseph Campbell

"In a job negotiation, the implementation of that deal is your success, which also leads to the company's success."

- Christopher Voss

So far, we have learned many traits of a Yes Man, and we have seen that these traits are beneficial in both your work and personal life. On one hand, they help you 'carve your niche' at work; on the other, they assist you in achieving a work-life balance at home. The world is filled with people who will agree with you, but there also exists a large number who do not. You can't ignore the fact that a significant portion of the world's population may not be amiable towards you. They may have different perspectives or viewpoints than yours. What may seem correct, appropriate, or rational to you may appear absurd to them. In such scenarios, how can you maintain your viewpoint and still be a Yes Man?

It's entirely possible to be a Yes Man even when those around you (such as colleagues, friends, or family members) hold different viewpoints than yours. To support my viewpoint, I would like to provide certain examples.

- Suppose your colleague wants his name to be prominently displayed or highlighted in bold for a particular assignment where you are also a team member. In this case, don't take things personally; rather, let things unfold naturally because, ultimately, it is the supervisor who will assess everyone's contributions.

- Suppose your boss reprimands one of your colleagues in your presence; remain neutral at that moment. You may later express your Yes Manship towards your colleague by accepting his friend request on social media, which has been pending, or by accepting his invitation to an informal gathering he has organised.

> These examples clearly demonstrate that a Yes Man is a very amiable, courteous, and understanding person who is not easily provoked and maintains a balanced demeanour.

Another trait that emerges from the above discussion is that a Yes Man allows things to happen. He lets things flow. He ensures that matters proceed smoothly unless there is a significant flaw in the proceedings.

A Yes Man delivers results and makes things come alive. There are people in every field who are persistent chain-blockers; they hinder progress regardless of how refined and flawless the actions may be. Such chain-blockers never allow things to function smoothly because of their intolerant and high-handed attitudes. It's not the 'project' which has been conceptualised by a team of experts that has suddenly appeared out of nowhere; rather, it has been proposed through extensive deliberations and sincere recommendations. While minor discrepancies may exist, they can often be rectified without much fuss. However, these chain-blockers have a habit of constantly nagging and creating mountains out of molehills.

> In summary, we can say that a Yes Man makes things flow, makes things happen, and brings ideas to life.

DOES A YES MAN SAY 'YES' TO EVERYTHING?

"When you say 'Yes' to others, make sure
you are not saying 'No' to yourself."

- Paulo Coelho

"Love yourself enough to set boundaries. Your time and
energy are precious. You get to choose how you use
your time. You teach people how to treat you
by deciding what you will and won't accept."

- Anna Taylor

By reading thus far, we understand that a Yes Man is not a weak person. He is committed to his work and is not distracted by the whims of others. He ensures that deliverables are met without fuss, producing positive results that benefit the company while safeguarding the interests of employees or subordinates.

However, the question that constantly bothers us is: does a Yes Man say 'yes' to everything?

We know that a Yes Man is a strong, methodical, and sincere person. His decisions hold significant weight for the supervisor and the company. It would not be an exaggeration to say that the Yes Man is the most dependable person in the company. The supervisor and management rely on him for their major stakes, whether financial, employee welfare, intercompany dealings, or legal issues. The management of the company values the decisions made or suggested by the individual we call a Yes Man.

When the Yes Man is such a dependable person, how can he blindly say 'yes' to everything? Very conclusively, I would argue that A YES MAN IS ALWAYS OPEN TO SAYING 'YES.' He is all ears to his boss, management, colleagues, and subordinate staff.

In other words, a Yes Man must be free from any kind of mental blocks and should act as a facilitator, never a chain-blocker.

The Yes Man is intrinsically motivated and full of positivity, which drives him to resolve matters without conflict and produce firm and substantive results. A Yes Man FINDS VALUE IN SAYING 'YES.' He appreciates Yes Manship and upholds this value to the highest order of thought. He takes pride in saying 'yes.'

YOU DON'T HAVE TO BE A COMPLETE YES MAN

This heading might seem ironic given what we've discussed so far, but beneath it all, we understand that a Yes Man is a facilitator, but not at the expense of honesty, ethics, or moral conduct.

Thus, I would like to slightly modify my statement about the Yes Man and assert with pride that 'you don't have to be a complete Yes Man.'.' What I mean is that the so-called Yes Man must be wise, witty, and fair when concluding agreements.

Simply nodding in agreement without using one's intellect can land you and the company in trouble, which is in NO WAY A WISE PERSON'S WORKMANSHIP.

SO, BE A WISE INCOMPLETE YES MAN,
OR A NOT-SO-COMPLETE YES MAN,
OR DON'T BE A FOOLHARDY, YES MAN.

Another great way to describe a Yes Man is that he says 'Yes' more often than others.

Come play a game with me. Let's burst our balloons of Yes Man-ship.

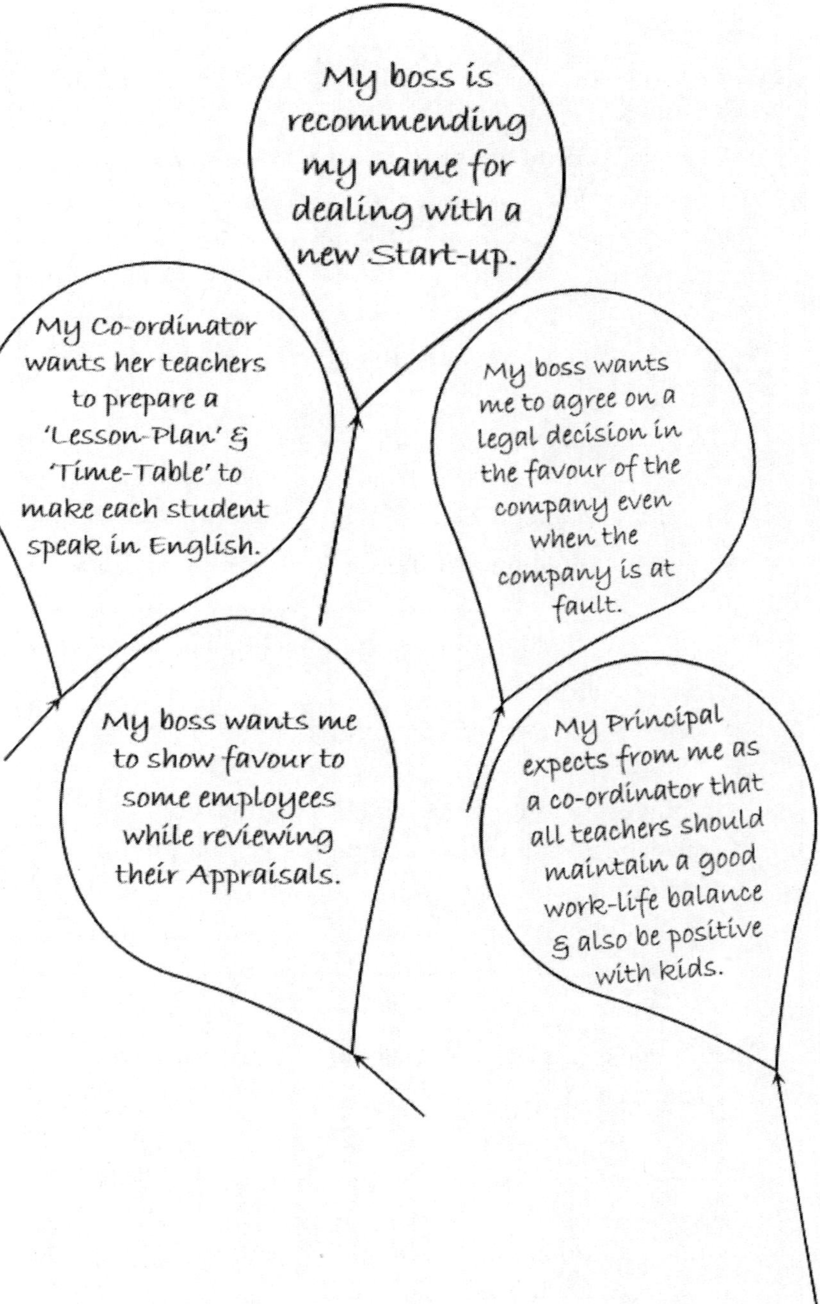
My boss is recommending my name for dealing with a new Start-up.
My Co-ordinator wants her teachers to prepare a 'Lesson-Plan' & 'Time-Table' to make each student speak in English.
My boss wants me to agree on a legal decision in the favour of the company even when the company is at fault.
My boss wants me to show favour to some employees while reviewing their Appraisals.
My Principal expects from me as a co-ordinator that all teachers should maintain a good work-life balance & also be positive with kids.

ACTIVITY 8

My Roadmap to 'Carve a Niche'

1. I'm a Yes Man because of these virtues ....
   ....
   ....
   ....
   ....

2. I feel there is no harm in being a Yes Man because
   ....
   ....
   ....
   ....

3. My goals are slightly different from others as I ....
   ....
   ....
   ....
   ....
   ....

4. My biggest quality as a Yes Man in both my professional and personal spheres is that I'm able to maintain a good ....
   ....
   ....
   ....

5. My biggest quality as a Yes Man in professional life is that I am a...
   ....
   ....and not a
   ....
   ....
   ....

Chapter Nine
Self Appraisal

SELF APPRAISAL: YOUR CHANCE TO SHOWCASE YOUR WORK

"It's not just about being better; it's about being different. You need to give people a reason to choose your business."

- *Anonymous*

"We don't learn from experience.
We learn from reflecting on experience."

- *John Dewey*

"Ask yourself if what you are doing today is getting you closer to where you want to be tomorrow."

- *Radmaverix*

In the previous chapters, we have explored numerous ways to 'Carve our Niche' in our professional sphere. We can discover our 'purpose for doing a job' and work diligently to hone our skills, which will help us reflect on our past experiences and better align ourselves with our current roles. We can identify our 'talents' and seek jobs that suit them. We should understand our value and face our worth to grow with confidence in our careers. We can fully leverage our 'professional attitudes' to 'Carve a Niche' whenever we choose to pick or switch jobs.

Once we have imbibed 'these professional qualities, we can take the lead in our roles and set the tone for our progression.

These methods, among many others, have been discussed in depth in the preceding chapters.

The objective here is not to enumerate all those methods that assist you in 'Carving Your Niche' but to focus on a larger point: whether incorporating these methods has created an impact on your supervisors. If so, how can that be commensurate with the effort you have invested in your work?

> The easiest way to make an impression on your supervisor is by critically presenting your achievements during the 'Self-appraisal' process at the end of the year.

Your self-appraisal reflects your duty-bound obedience, vision, wisdom, sincerity towards work, and, above all, the diligence you have demonstrated. It is perhaps the best way to highlight the work ethics and strategies you have followed throughout the year, setting a benchmark for the company.

Your self-appraisal is the only record that may remain firmly in your supervisor's mind, as it represents your best foot forward.

Your supervisor may not remember every detail of your work, but by reviewing your appraisal, they will recall the landmarks you established, the benchmarks you set, and the milestones you achieved for the company through your dedication and work ethic.

Your self-appraisal will be etched in your supervisor's memory and will influence their decisions regarding your future roles. It will serve as a blueprint for your upcoming assignments.

You will certainly be judged and, at the same time, be positively propelled into a new task based on your self-appraisal. Your self-appraisal becomes your report card for obtaining new assignments, better compensation, and a your-kinda ecosystem in future years.

> Your self-appraisal will lead you to greater heights in your career. It will become the guiding light for your professional development.

Filling out your self-appraisal is your opportunity to showcase your work throughout the year.

You may have accomplished many tasks over the year, but you might not remember every detail of the extensive responsibilities you undertook. Some of those forgotten tasks may hold significant importance for your future assignments. So, what can you do to recall such details? This query has already been addressed in the chapter on 'Documentation.' Yes! Documenting your work is the skill that will come to your rescue. You may want to revisit that chapter to grasp the nitty-gritty of documentation.

HOW TO FILL OUT THE SELF-APPRAISAL?

Now, suppose you've documented everything. The next question is: Is it possible to write every detail of your work in the self-appraisal? No way! It's not possible, nor is it even required.

Documentation is a very good practice, and I've even referred to it as a 'Necessary Evil.' This phrase captures the true value of documentation. If we don't need to present every task we've completed throughout the year, why is documentation given so much importance? The answer lies in the 'Documentation' chapter, but here I would like to remind you that documentation helps you, or you can say it saves you when you find yourself in troubled waters or need old records to substantiate your point. I hope you remember this...

So, while documentation is essential, how then are you required to fill out your self-appraisal? The only 'mantra' is to 'pose larger' while completing your self-appraisal. POSING LARGER does not mean you exaggerate your work; rather, it means you express your work beautifully.

EXPRESSION ALONE REVEALS YOUR DEDICATED AND DILIGENT WORK STYLE

So, what exactly do we mean by the word 'expression' here? Is it merely about using well-curated, well-articulated language, or does it involve something more?

True! Using appropriate language is important, but beyond that, 'expression' is an impactful way to present your work. It showcases everything about your working style, work ethic, vision, skills, accomplishments, and enthusiasm for your work.

'Expression' is a careful selection of your well-crafted work profile, which is self-explanatory and requires no further elaboration.

'Expression' serves as a true reflection of how you project yourself in your work sphere.

So, what should a self-appraisal look like? What should be the key points or keywords of your self-appraisal? What should be the central idea behind it? What should precisely become part and parcel of your entire self-appraisal?

> From our discussion so far, it is clear that you need to highlight those points that emphasise your work over the past year, as these will become the precursor to your future role in the company.

So, how do you write a self-appraisal? That is the point of contention.

Let me outline these points of contention below:

- You might consider writing only your major achievements.
- You might focus solely on your significant accomplishments.

- You might boast about your work to create an indelible mark on your supervisor.
- You might ignore the less significant tasks.
- You may include only the significant works, which project our projecting your image in a larger-than-life perspective.
- You may tend to write about our your achievements as they are, without mentioning the influence or impact they had on the company's growth.

So, what is the correct way of writing to write a self-appraisal, or what is the best way of writing the appraisal approach to ensure an everlasting impact? What are those small things that should be taken care of? How can we make our appraisal sound musical and not harmonious rather than cacophonous? What should be our working style so that our appraisal stands out and is earmarked for sending clarity and clearly conveys our vision, work style, and work ethic?

It's high time now that we crack down on we address some of the most daunting practices of writing a Self self-appraisal. Let's list them down here with some examples:

- Your self-appraisal should be brief, concise, and to the point. For example, you can write specifically about your targets achieved month-wise/week-wise/semester-wise/ or financial year-wise, and so on. Here, you can also mention the workshops/ seminars/ symposiums, you attended to upgrade or hone your skills during the aforementioned period. Here, you should include the name of the workshop, the educator or expert, and the outcomes of the workshop attended.

Workshops are always an integral part of any company or institution. They should be attended whenever possible, as they guide you in advancing your career. Since they are conducted by experts, they help you reach out to your audience or examine your job nuances critically. Such workshops help you build upon your existing knowledge and prioritise the course of future teaching or advancements in the company.

As a school teacher and coordinator, I attended numerous workshops on topics like 'easy teaching-learning techniques in a classroom.'.' One technique that impressed me greatly is the 'Mnemonic' technique, which is explained below:

For example, students can easily remember the names of the planets using this method. The eight planets, in order of their distance from the Sun, are Mercury, Venus, Earth, Mars, Jupiter, Saturn, Uranus, and Neptune. Kids can learn these names effortlessly using the Mnemonic technique.

Let's write down the first letter of each planet's name: M, V, E, M, J, S, U, and N. Now, we can frame a meaningful sentence using these letters:

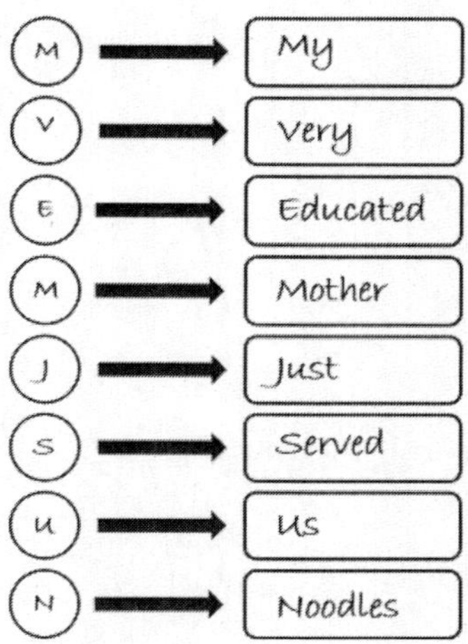

When we read the whole sentence 'together, it becomes: 'My very educated mother just served us noodles.'

Now, let's return to the point where we stated that our appraisal should be brief, concise, and to the point. For this, you should mention all the significant milestones achieved during the year, including workshops where you learned new and innovative methods to enhance your performance. Your milestones may include participation as a teacher, employee, or supervisor in various extracurricular or external affairs such as interschool competitions, field trips, sports day, or annual events. In office administration, you might have engaged in making presentations before clients, dealing with new partners, or managing financial transactions with banks or partner companies. Such responsibilities can be substantial and will depend on your position and work profile within the company.

In short, you need to highlight in your appraisal the 'stakes' you took for the company's or institution's benefit.

SOME MORE TIPS FOR WRITING AN APPRAISAL

"An ounce of performance is worth pounds of promises."

- *Mae West*

"I am the measure of my worth. And I say I am worthy."

- *Good Therapy.org*

Let's explore additional tips for writing a self-appraisal. The self-appraisal should emphasise the positive aspects of your work, while the negative aspects should be avoided. Your appraisal is a reflection of your work profile; it should demonstrate how hard and smartly you work to elevate your company to the next level. It should highlight your strengths and avoid your weaknesses unless specifically requested.

If the 'Appraisal Form' asks you to mention a bit about your weaknesses, you should be clever in how you handle it. You may discuss a common weakness that many employees share, presented candidly, along with a redressal procedure. You can mention the steps you've taken to overcome those weaknesses and how, through your wisdom and proactive nature, you turned them into strengths.

Your supervisor should never perceive you as having a particular weakness or shortcoming that hinders your performance. Instead, they should feel that any weaknesses you possess are far outweighed by the remedies and prompt decisions you make.

Your supervisor should always see that you prioritise the company's interests in your actions, reflecting your strengths. They should find you dependable for the company under all circumstances, regardless of any weaknesses you may have. Your weaknesses should never linger in any dark corner of your supervisor's mind. Never give your supervisor the slightest inkling of your weaknesses, as this could negatively impact your career.

> In summary, you should be able to highlight your strengths impactfully in your appraisal and discuss your weaknesses with complete command, focusing on the progress you've made.

Your self-appraisal should showcase your efficiency and promptness in completing the various tasks assigned to you, as well as how energetically you performed. It should also highlight that you executed your assigned tasks and those for which you took the initiative. Your readiness to uphold any stake should be reflected in your self-appraisal. For this, you need to indicate the time frame in which you achieved the targets. If you succeeded in completing any task before the stipulated time, you may mention the assigned date and the date of completion.

So, remember the four key qualities of any employee: EEPR (Efficiency, Energy, Promptness, Readiness). Any employee with good EEPR can be the next eligible candidate for promotion.

Let's discuss what I mean by EEPR, as it has become an interesting acronym:

- **E:** The first 'E' signifies that the employee should be 'efficient' in their work. This means the employee should be hardworking and capable of delivering results in less time than stipulated. Your appraisal should mention that all assigned tasks were completed much earlier than the given time (if you actually achieved this). Otherwise, you need to work on your efficiency to do well in your job.

- **E:** The second 'E' signifies your 'energy level' when completing any work. It correlates with your interest in a particular task. If you are interested in a project, your energy levels will be high, which will surely reflect in the quality of your work. Always save your energy for challenging tasks and approach them with enthusiasm. This will help build your reputation in the company and give you an edge over your colleagues. Now, the question is: how will you demonstrate your energy levels or quantify them? It's simple logic: energy levels equate to interest in work, and the outcome of that interest can be quantified by the number of targets or goals achieved, i.e., your contribution to improving the company's ranks in the audit list.

> So, energy levels can be quantified by measuring your interest, which is reflected in the growth of the company.

- **P:** The 'P' signifies showing 'promptness' in picking up work. This is a very important attribute of an employee. It highlights how quickly an employee understands a particular task, how fast they grasp the nuances of the task, and how effectively they bring it to a conclusion.

So, how will you quantify your promptness? Again, it can be equated to the outcome, which will be reflected in the number of assignments you picked up and brought to concrete conclusions.

- **R:** The 'R' signifies 'readiness'.' This reflects your zeal for completing a particular assignment. You may have taken on a task, but if you frequently approach your manager for clarification on the nuances, it reflects poorly on you. You must work hard to study the task or assignment in detail and gather as much information as possible from the internet and other sources. You are always expected to do your homework before discussing it with your manager. Thus, an employee needs to show readiness for work, and this should be articulated in your appraisal.

I'm sure you'll now be able to think of ways to quantify your readiness. You just need to consider how to quantify the outcome. What should be the result of demonstrating readiness at work? You'll perform better than colleagues who fail to prepare adequately. In this case, while the time taken to complete the task may be longer or the same as the one assigned to you, the accuracy of your work will reflect the quality of your performance.

> To quantify readiness, state in your appraisal that your job/task was near perfection and that you are well-equipped for future projects to be built upon this particular one. You can even assign grades based on the quality of your work, such as A +, A, B+, B, and C.

EEPR is not a standard measure for an employee, but I have devised it based on my job experiences.

ACTIVITY 9

My Roadmap to 'Carve a Niche'

1. I'll take full advantage of my..
....
....
....
....
...... [insert qualities] to fill out my Self-appraisal form
2. My appraisal should reflect my....................................
....
....
....
.... [insert qualities].
3. I'll leverage my ....
....
....
....
.... [insert qualities] throughout the year to remember the small details of my work.
4. I'll make my appraisal sound musical and not cacophonous by writing ....
....
....
....
.... [insert examples].
5. I'll ensure my appraisal is impactful in a way that paves the way for my future ....
....
....
....
.... [insert goals].

Chapter Ten
How To Get A Job?
(Part 1)

SEEDS FOR A CAREER ARE SOWN IN CHILDHOOD

"Before the reward, there must be labour.
You plant before you harvest. You sow in tears
before you reap joy."

- Ralph Ransom

"The law of harvest is to reap more than you sow."

- James Allen

"Our job is not the harvest; our job is the seed."

- Carl Lentz

We have discussed at length the 'Big Question' and the subsequent 'Tickling Question' in Chapter 1, but here I feel another fundamental question should be included in my book. It is one of the most important questions that lingers in our minds when we are in middle school or high school.

Let me first talk about the mindset with which a child enters school and slowly learns that they are being taught for a purpose beyond just becoming capable of reading and writing a particular language. They begin to understand that they were sent to school not just to be literate but to grasp much more than rudimentary studies.

Common questions arise, such as: "Why am I passing a class every year when the number of classes seems never-ending?" "Where is the end to all the subjects I have been learning day in and day out?" and, "Can I ever get over this burden one day?"

These questions are basic and quite natural, stemming from a tender, immature, pure, and blank mind that has just emerged from the cradle of its mother's arms and is now subjected to a seemingly harsh environment. The mind of a child needs to be nurtured with the utmost care and attention. A child who only knew about their parents or perhaps a sibling is now suddenly part of a class of 20 to 30 peers. This transition itself puts great pressure on the child's tender brain. However, eventually, the child begins to flutter their wings and opens up in a cordial atmosphere, where they start receiving nourishment for the brain. As they begin to acquire knowledge, the windows of their mind open to let in the air that will satisfy their thirst for answers to the immense questions their newfound knowledge has brought them.

Probably, the seeds of a career are being sown at this time, and once the right seeds are sown, a good harvest is inevitable. Therefore, a child should be treated in the most gentle, warm, and caring environment. School is the place where questions are answered in a satisfying manner that encourages children to learn more, a place that does not hinder their doubts from being expressed; a place that gives wings to their imagination and aspirations.

Much of this is addressed by our education policies and the ever-evolving education system, which is and should always be child-centred rather than curriculum-centred. In our formal education system, a child of 3+ years enters formal schooling, beginning their 'educational career' from nursery and kindergarten, progressing to primary, middle, high, and senior secondary school. This hierarchy has been carefully designed after a great deal of thought, considering numerous factors such as the child's brain development, psychomotor skills, visual skills, and many other aspects of a child's growth.

Once children become an integral part of the education system, they learn and develop numerous skills in school. In addition to learning how to read, write, and speak, the child also acquires skills in arts, music, dance, easy math calculation techniques (like Abacus, Vedic Math, etc.), computer skills, good behaviour and manners, language and literature, scientific skills, and so on. These skills and attributes are so valuable that they become part of a child's identity.

Having been equipped with such a variety of skills, a child can pick any area of interest, develop it, and pursue higher studies in that field to grow organically and pave the way for a bright future. In this way, once the foundation for a future career has been laid in school, the rest becomes history.

HOW TO GET THE JOB YOU WANT?

"Let the beauty of what you love be what you do."

- Rumi

"Pleasure in the job puts perfection in the work."

- Aristotle

"The best way to appreciate your job is to
imagine yourself without one."

- Oscar Wilde

So far, we have discussed that the seeds of a career are sown in childhood when a child is exposed to knowledge in school. It is not that the child is inadvertently or forcibly made to study; they are sent to school to acquire knowledge and to be able to fend for themselves in the future. In the beginning, we hardly consider the child's likes and dislikes. While in school, a child is guided to learn various subjects and is expected to excel in all of them equally, both by parents and teachers.

As children grow, they often develop a special interest in a particular subject. They are most excited to attend the class that satisfies their cognitive thirst. They cannot be blamed for showing over-enthusiasm for one subject over another.

Why are children overwhelmed when that particular class or period begins?

Children feel overwhelmed by a particular subject for numerous reasons. They might appreciate the particular style or manner in which that subject is taught by a specific teacher who excels in that subject. However, the primary reason is often their ZEAL FOR THAT SUBJECT. It's the brain power that draws children to that subject. If the teacher is dedicated, it's the 'cherry on the cake.'

So, what I mean to emphasise is that it's crucial for parents to identify the subject or area of a child's interest. By now, parents often recognise their child's likes and dislikes regarding subject choices.

I stress this point because once the 'area of interest' of a child is identified with the help of parents and teachers, 50% of the work toward a brighter future for the child is accomplished. The remaining 50% will be taken care of by the child's future education.

It's essential to identify a child's area of interest early, as doing so makes the journey to a successful career much easier.

NEVER PUSH OR BURDEN YOUR CHILD WITH A SUBJECT THEY ARE NOT INTERESTED IN

Once the 'Area of Interest' of a child is identified with the help of parents and teachers, I believe that half the work toward a good career is done. I still stand by my statement, but is it really as simple as determining a child's area of interest? The answer is 'No.'

In the early years of education, children are often too young and naive to understand the importance of selecting subjects of interest from a broader perspective. Schools teach all subjects until grade 10, and students are expected to perform well in every subject. Consequently, children feel significant pressure when deciding on subjects based on their interests.

In addition, parents often exert pressure, trying to force their children to pursue the so-called 'elite subjects'—a term I introduced in previous chapters—in their efforts to fulfil their aspirations.

The term 'Elite Subjects' refers to subjects such as science, math, commerce, and economics. Most parents don't want their children to take up arts, history, geography, or languages (at least the majority of parents) as their primary choice because they have a strong inner desire to see their children becoming doctors, engineers, or chartered accountants. They feel that the future of their children is more secure with these professions. These traditional professions hold high value in our parents' minds for financial reasons, as they are highly paid.

However, during the past few years, there has been a shift among parents from traditional courses to new courses that are being recognised in our society without forsaking financial aspirations.

Some of these courses include fashion design, mass communication, journalism, fine arts, BBA, MCA, B.Ed, M.Ed (Bachelor and Master in Education), B.Lib, M.Lib (Bachelor and Master in Library), LLB, LLM (law courses), M.Phil, PhD (Master and Doctor of Philosophy), data analysis, content creation, Visharad degree in music, NSD courses to fulfil acting ambitions, dance courses, etc.

I want to emphasise that you shouldn't burden your child with a subject they are not interested in; rather, motivate and educate them about other avenues based on their interests. It's clear from our in-depth discussion that if a child chooses a subject they are interested in for higher education, they are likely to rise to greater heights in their future career.

It's also evident that with the advent of new educational research, various diverse fields of study have emerged, catering to children's interests by helping them develop and hone their skills, thereby consolidating their positions in their careers.

GO FOR ACCLAIMED SKILL-ORIENTED COURSES

"The future belongs to those who learn more skills and combine them in creative ways."

— Robert Greene

"Repetition is the mother of skill."

— Tony Robbins

"Knowledge is not skill. Knowledge plus ten thousand times is a skill."

— Shinichi Suzuki

The above quotes emphasise the importance and value of skill development. It has already been hinted in this book that numerous courses are available today, aside from traditional ones. These courses have been devised considering the child's abilities and areas of interest.

In this chapter, it has been discussed that no subject of study should be forced upon a child; rather, the child should be encouraged and provided with all resources to pursue their choice of subjects or courses.

Various reasons, points of view, and several supporting statements have been made in previous pages, which speak highly of the importance of choosing subjects related to a child's area of interest.

Once the tone is set for the right academic course or subject, there is no way the child's career cannot be safeguarded, nor is their future predetermined. THE RIGHT DECISION AT THE RIGHT TIME CAN HELP FACILITATE MANY FUTURES.

Now, did you realise that while repeatedly discussing a child's area of interest, we have hit the nail on the head?

Yes, the subjects or courses related to one's area of interest are called 'skill development courses.' So, now we can easily define 'skill' before knowing which courses could be designated based on the so-called skill.

Skill is nothing but mastering any single work or job. Skill means developing the abilities or capabilities to perform any job with the highest degree of knowledge and interest. When choosing a career, you might have to learn one or more skills because, as I mentioned, for every single job in a field, you will need to learn a specific skill.

Let's understand this with a simple example.

To converse fluently with people, you need to learn communication skills. To achieve great communication skills, one must learn to read, write, and speak a particular language. To develop fluency in communication, one needs to master grammatical skills, semantics, and certain idioms and proverbs to make articulation more effective.

In a way, you can say that to learn a particular skill (for example, communication skills), one must grasp many relevant skills related to it.

That's the reason I say that a child cannot excel in all subjects or respond equally well in every subject because each subject demands learning or grasping numerous skills.

To quote Shakespeare: "A jack of all trades is a master of none." This means that a person could have diverse knowledge but may not be an expert in any particular skill. These days, it's no longer enough to just have basic knowledge. Every field, whether it's business, hospitality, medical care, engineering, or something else, needs experts.

We derive from the above discussion that mastering any one particular skill or becoming a specialist in a specific skill is much more in demand in the current world compared to someone who has done 'General Studies.'

In today's world, we have also seen that skill-oriented courses are emerging swiftly and becoming more popular than traditional courses of study. Skill-oriented courses target a particular area of study with a focus on specifics and cater to a very specific group of people, companies, or job types.

What I emphasise is that these skill-oriented courses generate a set of specialists who cater to the specific needs of the people. For example, the 'fashion designing' course will produce fashion designers who will serve the fashion industry. These students will be experts in designing and making clothes. Students who choose this course must have an artistic, creative, and imaginative temperament, along with great motor skills throughout their studies.

So, pursuing a course that shapes their inherent skills is the first step toward a fruitful career.

We have heard the saying, "One must follow his interest or passion." This statement is a bit hypocritical in the sense that people often study something else for their careers and then use their post-retirement time to follow their passion. How nice it would be if people did what they said or if PEOPLE PRACTISED WHAT THEY PREACHED!

> There has been a revolution in the field of education, and nowadays, the above statement is no longer hypocritical. With the advent of skill-oriented courses, more and more students are opting for courses that align with their passions or interests from the very beginning.

Briefly, I would like to give you an account of the various dynamic fields of study, apart from traditional courses, that children are choosing, as these courses are skill-oriented and offer promising careers in the future.

Examples of Skill-Oriented Courses

- Web development courses like JavaScript and HTML
- Data science and machine learning courses like Python, SQL, algorithms
- Cybersecurity courses like ethical hacking, cryptography
- Management courses like SEO, project planning, marketing, analytics
- Financial courses like Excel, valuation
- Graphic designing courses like Photoshop, UX/UI design
- Photography courses like DSLR camera operation, photo editing
- Video production courses
- Nursing courses
- Medical coding and billing courses
- Medical technician courses
- Vocational courses like electrician training

These are just some of the many acclaimed skill-oriented courses. The list is extensive and can be easily found online. These courses have been mentioned to encourage parents and children to think outside the box and move away from traditional lines of study.

DON'T OPT FOR SIMPLE ACADEMIC COURSES UNLESS YOU AIM TO BECOME AN ACADEMICIAN IN THE FUTURE

"Education is our passport to the future, for tomorrow belongs to the people who prepare for it today."

— Malcolm X

"The difference between education and know-how is that one you pay for, while the other you charge for."

— Robert Breault

The quote above emphasises that know-how is something you charge for, meaning a career provides monetary benefits. So, choose your career very carefully, and as we mentioned before, it should be chosen based on your area of interest.

We are going to discuss how skill-oriented courses have an edge over traditional academic courses.

We all know that the culmination of any course of study is the amount of money or the basic salary it can yield. We discussed in detail in Chapter 1 that people have different purposes for pursuing a job. Whatever the purpose, the basic mentality or mindset that keeps us going in a job is the 'bucks' we earn in return for our work.

It is certain that we all look for how well-paying our jobs are in the back of our minds. Somewhere down the line, we all seek a sophisticated package at the end of our education, setting aside the purpose of why we are doing the job in the first place.

We all want a handsome salary at the end of our education because the success of our life story depends on the amount of money earned by us at the end of every quarter.

It's a different story, and life's success depends on many other factors as well, which we won't delve into here, as that would start another chapter in life's story.

But, surely, money is one big factor in our success story. Now, keeping our focus on the 'money factor,' we can say that careers are linked to it. Everyone wants to choose a well-paying career.

So, let's tie together the threads of the discussion. We discover an important fact: SKILL-ORIENTED COURSES DEFINITELY PAY OFF WELL, AND THEY GENERALLY HAVE A DEFINED PERIOD OF STUDY.

Skill-Oriented Courses

- Teach you specific skills
- Provide know-how in a particular field
- Make you an expert or specialist in your field
- Are shorter in duration
- Open up many career opportunities
- Pay well

However, some students have different preferences and interests. They wish to pursue full academic courses later in life. They aim to be graduates, postgraduates, and then pursue doctorates, i.e., they want to continue higher studies in their field. They may wish to study science or arts and engage further by opting for research in their chosen subjects. That's a different mindset, approach, and way of shaping their studies.

I'm not advocating against pursuing such lines of study; rather, my aim is to highlight the 'cons' of traditional academic courses.

Conventional Academic Courses are

- Not skill-oriented
- Long, requiring a significant period to complete
- Culminate in research, making them heavy and time-consuming
- Potentially expensive, requiring many years of perseverance to achieve desired results
- They might lead to lower-paying jobs, such as stipends or scholarships

I am not opposed to conventional academic courses, but my objective in this chapter was to help students find career-oriented paths that also pay well. It's actually debatable whether one should opt for skill-oriented or conventional academic courses. Again, it's a matter of choice for students, which they'll eventually make based on their area of interest.

It's clear that without research in various fields, progress in technology, medical science, or other sectors would not be possible. And research is made possible only through conventional academic courses. Moreover, progress is impossible without the inventions and innovations that research facilitates.

How To Get A Job?
(Part 2)

INDULGE IN NETWORKING AFTER COMPLETING STUDIES

"Networking is marketing. Marketing yourself, your uniqueness, what you stand for."

— Christine Comaford Lynch

"Networking is an investment in your business. It takes time and, when done correctly, can yield great results for years to come."

— Diane Helbig

What do we mean by networking? I hope we all understand the basic meaning. Networking, in simple terms, means connecting with people, sharing ideas, projecting yourself, and so on. So why am I stressing the importance of networking while discussing career choices, courses, academic subjects, and job prospects?

It's obvious that after completing your studies, you will be looking for a suitable job. When you finish your studies, your know-how is strong, and your knowledge is fresh and theoretical. After completing your studies, your mind is like a blank slate, written solely with bookish knowledge. I call it a 'Blank Slate' because there is no practical or experiential knowledge written on it. A person without practical knowledge is like a bird without wings or a bird that cannot fly.

So, to give wings to your career path, you need to grow wings of practical knowledge. The importance of practical knowledge is so vivid and profound that a person with just his experiences in the subject can lead and glide over someone who has only book knowledge. We have all heard the idiom, "Practice makes a man perfect." It holds very true when marching forward in your career journey.

In the following histogram diagram, I have tried to explain the 'power of practice.'

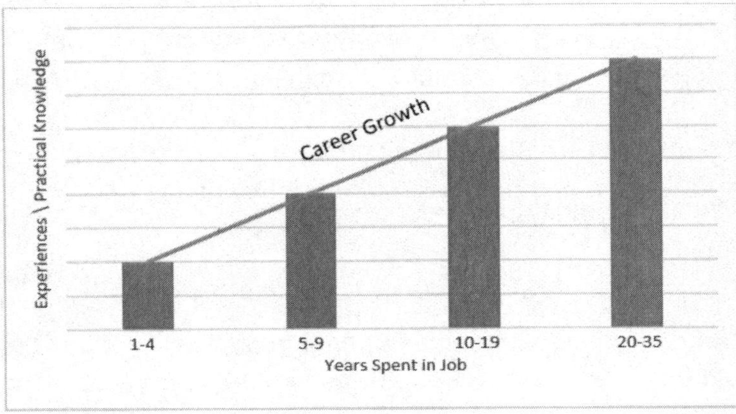

Once you are well-versed in practical knowledge, you can showcase your skills when applying for a job. To become proficient in practical knowledge, you must apply for some kind of apprenticeship or internship to enhance your experience.

After your internship, you can apply for jobs at various companies that come to the campus for recruitment. You may even make use of the referrals you have obtained through your networking. This is where networking plays a crucial role.

I will now share a few ways to 'network' based on my experience with my sons during their early career struggles:

1. Networking is an ongoing process that may start as early as childhood.
2. Maintain relationships with good-natured, open-minded, and helpful people you meet in life. They can be valuable connections in your network.

3. You can even connect with highly accomplished people who were impressed by your work style at some point. They will always remember you for your uniqueness.
4. When career fairs are held on campus, participate and try to make a lasting impression on recruiters through your interpersonal skills, knowledge, and acumen.
5. You can also get referrals from recruiters at career fairs or from seniors who have established themselves in their jobs.
6. In essence, networking is about maintaining cordial interpersonal relationships that you can build during your college days and beyond.
7. You must also project your USP (Unique Selling Proposition), which we will discuss in the next few pages, to help you become a sought-after candidate by recruiters.
8. Networking results from your extroverted, eloquent, and sociable traits, which will significantly impact your career when continuously developed.
9. Networking is possible with like-minded individuals who share common interests and experiences with you.
10. Networking is also possible with people who were in a similar situation to yours but have since moved on. They can still relate to you and are open to offering guidance and help.

So, we can say that networking is an essential part of our lives while we are studying and also when we are done with our studies and looking for a job.

IT IS NECESSARY TO PROJECT YOURSELF

"Anybody who becomes a movie star becomes successful at projecting a certain image to the public."

— Jay McInerney

"Projecting a persuasive image of a desirable and practical future is extremely important to high morale, dynamism, consensus, and, in general, to help the wheels of society turn smoothly."

— Herman Kahn

In today's world, which is full of individuals with unique skills in various fields, it is essential to project your qualities, skills, and uniqueness to the world. There has been a sudden rush of talent in various fields as more and more students join the race to secure jobs. In the past, there were fewer fields of study, and not everyone had the opportunity to study due to low literacy rates. With the advent of the new age, industrialisation, and modernisation of societies, everyone, regardless of background, now has a fair chance to access education.

These days, we find children from humble backgrounds also securing high-ranking jobs in society because they have ample opportunities for education. Education is no longer a barrier to the success story of any child. Every Indian and child worldwide is getting an equal share of education and access to higher education, irrespective of their background. This has become possible because the light of literacy has illuminated every nook and corner of our country and the world.

As a result, the world has become so competitive. So, how do I project myself as the best candidate for a particular job? This is a question that will cross every student's mind after finishing college. And the answer is quite simple, although it might not seem so straightforward. If you have completed a specific skill-oriented course, you possess unique knowledge and practical know-how in that area. This is where you have an edge over other students, even those specialised in the same skill.

> So, you can project yourself based on your skill, which is unique to you. In a way, you have to SELL YOUR UNIQUENESS TO THE WORLD to secure the place you deserve in the job market.

The modern world calls it the USP. You have to tell the world that this is my USP (Unique Selling Proposition) to brand yourself.

I hope the meaning of USP is crystal clear by now.

There will be many college graduates with the same degree, diploma, or certification or who have mastered the same skill-oriented course as you. So, how will you showcase your USP when applying for a job? Let me give you an example: There are 11 players in a cricket team, and all these sportsmen have undergone training to learn cricket. Each player learns the rules of the game and all the skills involved, such as batting, bowling, fielding, wicket-keeping, and catching. But how is it that some players excel at bowling and become great spinners, while others excel at batting and master strokes?

So, what I mean is that each player has acquired a different skill in which he is interested and which gives him the greatest pleasure and satisfaction, even though all 11 players had undergone training for the same sport. The same rationale holds for any course of study as well. Likewise, out of a batch of students passing the same course, each student will be good at some skill or another; that skill is his choice and interest. THAT SKILL BECOMES HIS USP.

Now, the candidate can use his USP to secure a job. With a USP in hand, getting a job will be much easier.

WHAT CAN I DO WITH MY USP?

Now that you have your USP in hand, you can do wonders with it. Your USP shows that you are an expert or specialist in that particular field. Now, you have to sell this uniqueness of yours in the market. The job market is a broad term that incorporates or can absorb a large number of potential candidates. Like in a jigsaw puzzle, only when the right piece fits in the right groove is the puzzle complete; so it is with getting the right job. When your résumé fits or catches the eye of the right recruiter, things fall into place, and you get the job of your choice.

Here are some tips on how you can make the best use of your USP:

- You must project your USP whenever you meet a recruiter or whenever you are networking.
- At career fairs, first survey the companies that have participated and what kind of skills they are looking for.
- You can mould your résumé in several ways depending on the type of jobs the companies are offering.
- You need to grasp the company's requirements and orient yourself in that direction.
- Leverage social media, LinkedIn, etc., to create a compelling presence for your USP that attracts the attention of many recruiters.
- You can even have a personal website where you can showcase your USP.
- Articulate your USP in such a way that your strong points or areas of knowledge and skill are highlighted.
- Approach mentors and peers who match your USP.
- Build a strong personal brand with your USP so that you can capture the job market with your uniqueness.

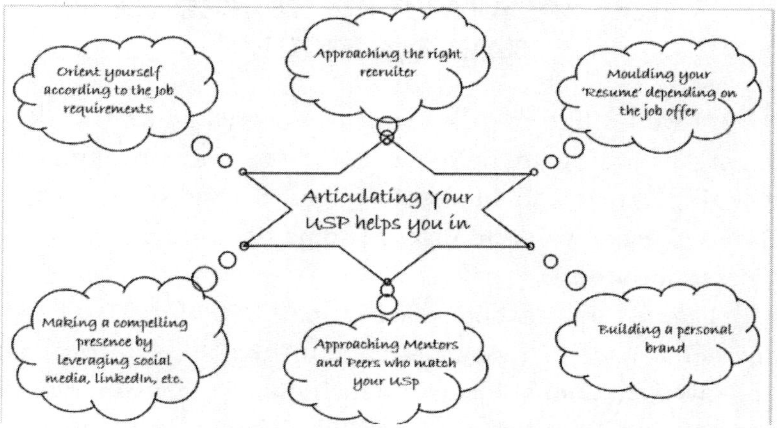
Orient yourself according to the Job requirements
Approaching the right recruiter
Moulding your 'Resume' depending on the job offer
Articulating Your USP helps you in
Making a compelling presence by leveraging social media, linkedIn, etc.
Approaching Mentors and Peers who match your USp
Building a personal brand

HOW MY BRANDING HELPED ME CARVE A NICHE

Here, I would like to talk about how I created and worked on my branding to help me make my way through my teaching career and successfully 'carve a niche' for myself. This will guide you and provide some tips on how to create a personal brand.

I joined as a school teacher in 1999. When I started, my mentors weren't very clear about my USP. As a result, I was given random subjects to teach. Slowly, my supervisors realised that I had a good command of the English language. However, to test my knowledge, I was given random notebooks from a class and asked to recheck them. I diligently followed the orders and rechecked those notebooks. That exercise proved to be a game-changer for me, and I was made a full-fledged English teacher.

My branding as a good English teacher later helped me secure a job in a reputed public school. My educational qualifications also clearly reflect my science knowledge, and I was easily assigned to teach science as well. Talking of my USP, I was now an accomplished science and English teacher. Alongside teaching, I was also very active in extracurricular activities. There were several inter-house competitions in my school, where my 'house' won several accolades under my guardianship.

I was later put in charge of the 'English Dramatics Club' at my school, where I scripted many plays and helped students showcase their talent in wonderful ways. With a background in zoology, I was also put in charge of the 'Birdwatching Club' at my school. During my tenure as a teacher, I got several opportunities to showcase my skills. I helped students organise science and various other exhibitions at school. I also prepared students for Science

Talent Search Examinations, elocution, debates, quizzes—the list is endless. With these and many more feathers in my cap, I was made the 'School Coordinator' early in my school career.

This is how I kept branding myself and adding to my USP, which allowed my career to grow.

I have quoted this simple real-life example to practically guide readers in continuously building their USP. Let me make it clear for new entrants: Initially, you might start with a few USPs to secure a job. But, with time, your USP will grow, and you can always leverage it to advance in your career.

ACTIVITY 10

My Roadmap to 'Carve a Niche'

1. I'll find out my 'area of interest' and will assist my children in finding their area of interest because this will help in ....
....
....
....

2. I will select ....
....
-oriented courses or ....
.... oriented courses depending on my interests and liking.

3. I'll indulge in networking after my studies and also during my studies because it helps in ....
....
....
....
....
....

4. It is very important to project your ....
....
....
....
....
....to get a job.

5. My USP would help me in building my personal ......
....
....
....
....

Chapter Eleven
Modern Work Culture

"The secret of success is, to be ready for
opportunities when they come."

- Benjamin Disraeli

"It is human nature to make decisions based on emotions rather than fact, but nothing could be more illogical."

- Toshiba Corporation

"If you do not invest in long term, there is no short term."

- George David

Life is not a bed of roses. It's full of challenges. You will face many defeats in life, but never feel yourself be defeated in life. I highly believe in Bhagwat Gita for lessons about life and situations. I follow ethics, Indian ethos and moral values in my personal and professional life. I always try to undertake and complete the job with utmost sincerity as per the law of the land in the best interest of all the stakeholders, including the nation at large. If your intent is good and you adhere to the right path at every moment, you don't need to bother about the result, you will really enjoy every moment of your journey.

I always take a challenge as an opportunity. There should always be a balance between the intellect and the emotions. Your good emotions will guide you to be on virtuous path and your intellect will help you in planning your mission and vision and eventually will help in the achievement of your goal and objectives in the life. As we know that every one of us wants to be happy in life. The happiness is derived from success, but the definition of success is different for different individuals depending upon the nature, profession and inbuilt software of the individual. So, in whatever field you are and if you desire to be successful, it requires meticulous planning, strategy and implementation with total quality management.

I've been in the field of urban infrastructure planning and development for the last 40 years and would like to share my experiences with you to help you gain insights to build a roadmap for success in your career.

PLANNING IS FOUNDATION OF EVERYTHING

"Our goals can only be reached through a vehicle of a plan, in which we must fervently believe and upon which we must vigorously act. There is no other route to success."

—Pablo Picasso

"A man who doesn't plan long ahead will find trouble at his door."

-Confucius

In general, planning is;
What to do?
How to do?
Who will do it?
When to do?

You may have more than one option to choose from, but what is most appropriate for you as per your core competencies, you should first identify that one project or field to work upon. Now, how to implement the plan?

Select a person or set of persons to complete the job within given cost and time frame. As a process, we have to arrange the various activities in the sequence and have to assign various resources and time for each activity. There may be some activities which may be undertaken parallel or simultaneously. Applying various techniques like CPM (Critical Path Method) and PERT (Program Evaluation And Review Techniques), the project may be completed within minimum time and cost.

There should be focused planning. In strategic planning, available resources are deployed to achieve the objective of the organisation. In operational planning, efficient use of the allocated and deployed resources is achieved. In tactical planning, which may be short range up to one year, medium range 1-3 years and long range from 3-10 years, plans may be made depending upon the nature of the project. The cost of any infrastructure project will be the sum of all the required resources to complete the project, which includes money, material, manpower, land, and technology. In most of the infrastructure projects, land is a major component. The use of the locally available building material reduces the cost. Use of latest technology and machines significantly reduces the time and cost of the project.

MANAGEMENT THE KEY FOR SUCCESSFUL IMPLEMENTATION OF THE PROJECT

"Management is above all, a practice where art, science, and craft meet."

-Henry Mintzberg

"Management is efficiency in climbing the ladder of success; leadership determines whether the ladder is leaning against the right wall."

—Stephen Covey

In general, we know that to get the work done from others is management, or a group of managers is the management, or a process of converting 5Ms (money, material, machines, etc.) into goods and services by planning, organising, directing and controlling is management.

We know that good management is only possible through great leadership.

The style of leadership of management in any organisation can be: (1) Autocratic or authoritarian, or (2) Free Rein, or (3) Participative or Democratic.

To my philosophy and understanding, participative or democratic leadership is the best as it has the folllowing advantages over the other two types of leaderships.

(i) There is more cooperation between the management and the employees.

(ii) There are less complaints and grievances between the management and the employees.

(iii) There is more acceptance of management ideas.

(iv) There is more sincerity and devotion of employees towards the job.

(v) The moral of the employee is generally higher.

Even when the participative leadership is the most congenial for an employee, but one has to be prepared for different atmospheres of the organisations. One can't just bank upon one type of leadership style. Career is a long journey with immense upheavals that demand adjustments to various localised atmosphere of the companies. For this one has to know on what factors such climate will depend.

The 'Organisational Climate' depends upon:

(a) Type of structure of the organisation

(b) Type of leadership

(c) Interpersonal relationship

(d) Degree of trust and freedom

(e) Reward system, and

(f) Communication and conflict management

All the good organisations always try to recruit good managers. For surviving the varied oganisational climates one needs to possess good managerial skills. Good managerial skills are not only the requirements of the employee himself, but the recruiter or promoters of the company also demand the same. So, let's throw some light on **Qualities of the Good Managers:**

(a) Well educated with specific technical knowledge

(b) Properly trained as his skill is not inborn quality

(c) Leadership quality to manage a number of subordinates and colleagues

(d) Self confidence to be in a position to take decisions in all situations

(e) Maturity-emotionally, mature with balanced temperament

(f) Farsightedness and receptive to new ideas and technologies

(g) Human relations attitude, cooperative, and helping hand to colleagues and subordinates

(We have discussed 'skill', 'farsightedness', and 'attitude' at large in previous chapters)

WHAT A RECRUITER SEEKS AND WHAT YOU SHOULD SEEK

An organisation always tries to recruit or appoint candidates mainly of qualities mentioned in above paragraph. At the same time, the aspiring job seekers should also consider to apply in an organisation which suit them the most as per their nature to 'create a niche', and mutual growth in the organisation in the time to come. The young aspirants should always try to look for an organisation which is employee friendly, influenced with Japanese culture and equipped with latest technologies. Such modern organisation will provide you more freedom and opportunities to work with minimum restrictions and you will always feel more confident and secured. In such organisations, you will find less discriminations and will have equal rights and opportunities to climb the ladder. There are less conflicts between the management and the employees, and as and when a conflict arises, they get a better conflict resolution mechanism to address the issues.

What are certain other parameters that may give a broad idea about the culture of the company to decide, which company may suit you more? Given below are some of the important analysis and techniques used by big modern companies which a new entrant should consider before approaching for the recruitment.

HIGH RETENTION RATE IN COMPANIES PERFORMING SWOT AND PEST ANALYSIS

SWOT Analysis:

The big modern companies always do SWOT (strength, weakness, opportunities, and threats) analysis before launch of the new product. The organisation evaluates at microlevel the internal strength and weakness at the same time, also evaluates at macro level, the external environmental opportunities and threats for a particular product. After internal evaluation of all micro factors and also external political and other environmental macro factors, a holistic decision is taken which drastically reduces the chances of loss in the future and in turn giving more security of job and promotion prospects to the employees.

PEST Analysis:

Here the big companies evaluate external macro environmental factors i.e. political, economic, social, and technological which give a broad landscape and sustainability in the future. PEST analysis can be expanded to PESTLE to include legal and environmental analysis for strategic planning and decision.

TQM (Total Quality Management) and JIT (Just in Time) MOST SOUGHT AFTER WAY OF MANAGEMENT FOR SUCCESS OF A COMPANY

"There is no substitute for quality and no greater threat than failing to be cost competitive on a global basis. These are complimentary concepts, not mutually exclusive ones."

— Bill Saparito

"Getting quality results is not a short-term; 'Instant-pudding' way to improve competitiveness. Implementing total quality management requires hand-on, continuous leadership"

— Armand V. Feigenbaum

Now, all the modern global companies follow TQM and/or JIT process to achieve 'zero defect' for a continuous improvement and customer satisfaction. TQM is a habit or a culture of continuous quality improvement by involving all concerned in the process and no-one should be left, as we know that the strength of the chain is decided by the weakest link. Zero defect management is 'doing it right' in the first attempt. Once Hewlett Packard estimated that the cost of 'doing not right' in the first attempt was 25% to 30 % of the revenue. But subsequently with use of Six Sigma and other techniques it was found that the cost was reducing significantly and still some more companies are thriving to contain it under 5%.

TQM and JIT reduce the cost of production and defect percentage of the product and overall increase the productivity. The cost of quality is never so significant. As we all know the prevention cost is much less in comparison to correction of defects. The principle is like the traditional medical axiom, "Ounce of prevention is worth a pound of cure." In general, the relationship between the cost of prevention, correction, and failure maybe in ratio of 1:10:100. It is very easy to understand in terms of road repair, for example, if a small pothole of road is not repaired immediately, it will increase polynomially in due course of time and so will the cost of repair. This phenomenon may be depicted as following.

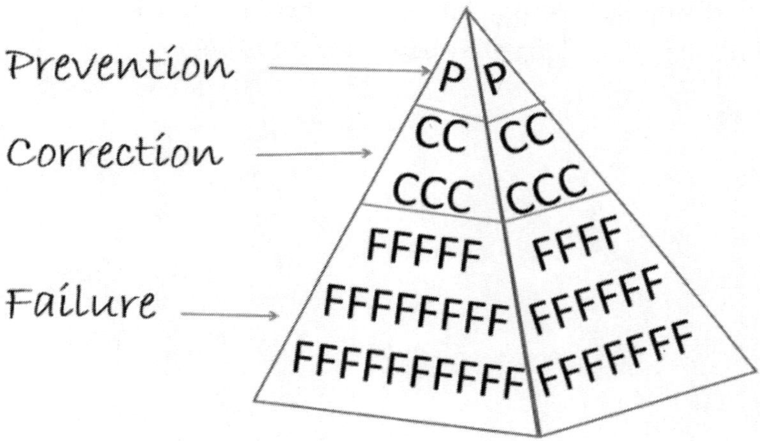

Based on the advantages, I would suggest the job seekers to go for the companies which follow TQM and JIT management techniques in the process to improve the quality and productivity.

GO FOR ISO- 9001 CERTIFIED COMPANIES

In globally competitive environment, there is no option but all the companies should comply with ISO (International Standard Organisation) standards to stay in the market. As of now some more than 1 million organisations are globally certified under ISO-9001.

ISO-9001 certified companies follow international standards for QMS (Quality Management Systems). The credibility and job satisfaction of employees in these companies is relatively high. The market opportunities are high and also provide better customer satisfaction. ISO-9001 certified companies get new contracts because of high credibility and trust and keep on expanding, so their financial growth is high. I, therefore, would like to recommend that ISO-9001 certified company should be the first choice for a job aspirant to join for better career growth opportunities. These companies may provide you better compensation and other benefits along with better work-life balance.

SIGNIFICANCE OF EMPLOYER BRAND AND COMPANY BRAND

The brand value of the company influences the career growth. It significantly help the candidates in getting better opportunities and leverage in other companies because of experience in such brand companies. The brand companies attract the top talent with good remunerations. The employees of these companies have better job satisfaction, good reputation and also good network, and good work-life balance. Good experience and better networking help them switch to better opportunities in other companies also.

Based on above attributes the brand value companies are good, but for young employees the 'Employer Brand' may be more beneficial in comparison to 'Brand Value'. The employer brand fosters more trust in job satisfaction and higher retention rate. In employer brand companies, the young employee finds more career options and workplace which suits to your values and cultures.

So, the young aspirants should seek companies of 'Employer Brand' and 'Brand Value' both, that too with more weightage to 'Employer Brand'. In this present social media time, the job seekers may validate the authenticity of the company from the testimonials and reviews of the company.

REENGINEERING IS THE NEW NORM

Earlier, most of the organisations remained committed to their labour specialisation, and typical structures, but now in the present global competitive and technological time it requires frequent restructuring and reorganisation. But many a times it is not cost effective and sustainable. So, now “Re-organising is out and Re-engineering is in” which means starting all over from Scratch. Yeah, I would like to suggest the new young graduates to prefer to start their career in a ‘Start up’ or New or ‘Re-engineered’ organisation where they will be valued more because of their latest updated knowledge and technology, and will be able to ‘create their Niche’ faster and will get better opportunities to rise the ladder.

In this chapter we have briefly described some of the best practices which most of the good companies follow for their sustainable growth. We have also outlined the requirements of the employer and of the young job seekers. According to the qualification and skill, one may plan and decide for himself the type of job, industry, and overall long term career goals.

As per your career goals, you may identify a company which is financially healthy, well-structured and of good work culture and environment, which provide you good compensation and other benefits along with good work-life balance and future growth opportunities.

Takeaways

- We should follow the righteous and virtuous path with a balance of intellect and emotions for building up our careers.
- Good planning is essential for successful completion of a project in minimum time and cost using the 'appropriate strategies' and 'latest techniques'.
- 'Participative leadership' leads to 'good management' with mutual trust and confidence between the 'employer' and the 'employees' and always yields best results.
- Young aspirants in order with their capabilities should go for' well-structured', 'brand value' and 'employer brand' companies or, 'Re-engineered' or 'Start-ups'.
- Preference may be given to 'ISO-9001' certified companies for better career growth with 'work-life balance'. You may find 'good work culture' and 'high productivity' in these companies because of the use of best practices and latest technologies.

AUTHOR BIOS

POONAM SINGH: The author of this book, Poonam Singh, is a published author and an educationist. Having graduated from the prestigious Miranda House, Delhi University in Zoology, the author realised her penchant for writing from her middle school days in Indian Community School, Tripoli Libya. She fondly celebrates her services as a school teacher and school coordinator, where she gave new dimensions to the teaching process in her capacity. Today she flaunts being a science blogger on YouTube and an active Instagrammer. With multiple live sessions on YT and IG, she never looked back and is all set to carry on her author journey with elan.

IP SINGH: The co-author of this book, IP Singh is a Gold Medallist technocrat from a central university of India with specialisation in Material Management, and Urban Planning and Development. He has worked in various positions in the government of UP and government of India, and presently working as a COO in a listed infra company of India.

He is an intellectual enthusiast, critical thinker, comprehensive expert, and passionate professional.

Connect with me

- Website- authorpoonamsingh.com
- Instagram- poonamsingh2764
- YouTube- Author Poonam Singh
- YouTube- SCIENCE BUG by Poonam Singh
- Facebook- Poonam Singh